SECRETS

OF A

HOLLYWOOD

PRIVATE EYE

A Rollicking
No-Holds Barred
Expose of Tinsel Town

FRED WOLFSON

WITH NEW YORK TIMES BESTSELLING AUTHOR

BURL BARER

WILDBLUE
PRESS

WildBluePress.com

SECRETS OF A HOLLYWOOD PRIVATE EYE
published by:
WILDBLUE PRESS
P.O. Box 102440
Denver, Colorado 80250

WILDBLUE PRESS is registered at the U.S. Patent and Trademark Offices.

ISBN 978-1-960332-03-5 Hardcover
ISBN 978-1-960332-02-8 Trade Paperback
ISBN 978-1-960332-04-2 eBook

Cover design © 2023 WildBlue Press. All rights reserved.

Cover Design by Tatiana Vila, www.viladesign.net
Interior Formatting by Elijah Toten, www.totencreative.com

SECRETS

OF A

HOLLYWOOD
PRIVATE EYE

Everything in this book is true. The names of some non-famous folks have been changed to protect their reputations. Celebrities' names have not been changed by us. Most of them had their names changed by their agents or managers.

INTRODUCTION

The world is not full of crooks and criminals. In truth, you are surrounded by kind, honest, decent people who will never lie, cheat, or steal without first failing the dual temptations of opportunity and justification.

Before a person can lie, thus beginning the progression that includes cheating and stealing, they must convince themselves that the deception is justified.

Some lies *are* justified. A doctor assuring a dying patient that they are on the path to recovery may be the positive deciding factor in life or death. When Nazis ask you if you have seen any Jews, and you have a family of four hiding in your attic, telling the truth would be an egregious sin. Malicious lying—giving false information with evil intent—is another matter.

Malicious liars steal the truth first, and then they steal possessions. Once you cross the line between truth and lies, the distinction between "yours" and "mine" is the next border breached.

Integrity erodes quickly or slowly depending upon the efficacy of justification, and this was tested by an interesting sociological experiment. A group of researchers entrusted people with one million dollars to hold safely for someone supposedly going out of the country for five years.

Only ten percent of the study's participants safeguarded the funds as agreed. The money, plus interest earned, returned untouched.

The majority—a whopping eighty percent—occasionally used some of the funds for financial emergencies or for granting themselves short-term loans. They justified these indiscretions because, at the end of the five years, they returned the full million.

The final ten percent stole all the money.

In another study, researchers set up a candy display in the middle of a supermarket. A hidden video camera allowed them to watch people help themselves without paying. The next day, they placed a guard in front of the display. The number of people helping themselves to candy dropped from six per hour to only one per hour. The one was the guard.

Conclusion: a primary characteristic of temptation is its ability to tempt. It is no coincidence that the Lord's Prayer says, "Lead us not into temptation, but deliver us from evil," acknowledging that most people, once tempted, lower their behavioral standards.

Theft is not always money. Sometimes it is time and/or emotions. When a spouse or lover cheats on you and then loots your bank account, the broken heart hurts more than the negative bank balance.

The number-one business loss is employee theft; the fastest-rising crime in America is identity theft. If you have money, someone wants to steal it or cheat you out of it.

It does not matter if you are poor or rich, famous or unknown. Actress Kate Beckinsale had her purse snatched while Christmas shopping in London; three men robbed an Amish family at gunpoint as they rode their horse-drawn buggy along a country road in northern Indiana.

When it comes to financial scams, people are most vulnerable when ignorant, and that includes Hollywood stars, producers, directors, and network executives. Rich and famous is not synonymous with investment savvy, nor does an absurdly large investment portfolio assure immunity to emotional and financial predators.

Former network news commentator Greta Van Susteren, actor Peter Coyote, and movie producer Armyan Bernstein (whose films include *Spy Game*, starring Robert Redford and Brad Pitt, and *Air Force One*, starring Harrison Ford) were among those entangled in an investment swindled by conman clergyman Reed Slatkin of the Church of Scientology.

"I wish I'd never met him," Bernstein told the *Los Angeles Times*. "He preyed on good people who were trusting."

"We were all stupid," said Greta Van Susteren's husband John Coale, a prominent Washington attorney. "I'm not a dummy. I went to school, but he got me on this one. Plus, I paid the asshole fees." Coale sympathized with the people who lost their life savings—he talked to a quadriplegic who gave Mr. Slatkin all her money. "I was ripped off too. I'm getting whooped at home, if you know what I mean," he said. "I'm not even allowed out of the house to buy cigarettes anymore. For a couple of years, I looked like an investment genius. Now I'm just a dope."

Catching and revealing a lying thief who takes advantage of people's trust and swindles them out of their life savings is one of the great joys of my career. A crooked executive in Los Angeles stole millions of dollars from investors, flew to Switzerland, and deposited the funds. His outraged victims confronted him with their accurate accusations; he insisted that he never went to Switzerland and he could prove it. They hired me to prove him wrong.

I had no idea what kind of proof he would offer, or how I would counter it. We sat down at a conference table, and he produced his proof—his passport.

"I never went to Switzerland," he insisted. "If I had, there would be an official Swiss stamp on a page in my passport. Go ahead. Look."

He handed me his passport. Sure enough, there was no Swiss stamp. Then, I silently counted the pages.

"Does anyone else in this room have a passport?" I asked. One of the other men had one. "Please be so kind," I asked, "to tell us how many pages are in a passport."

He carefully counted them. "Twenty-five," was his accurate response.

"*All* passports are twenty-five pages," I confirmed. "Yours, sir," I said to the crooked executive, "has only twenty-four pages. One page is missing—the page you removed because it had a Swiss stamp."

It was like a scene out of *Perry Mason*. He was drop-jawed. I got up, collected my fee of three thousand dollars, and walked away knowing I had exposed a criminal. He was guilty as hell and thought he could get away with it by tearing a page out of his passport. He was charged and convicted in a court of law. While it was comforting to his victims, they never recovered all their funds or their self-respect.

All of his victims were supposedly smart people. If it can happen to them, it can happen to you, especially if you are greedy.

The principal factor in any scam is greed. Without greed, you won't have a victim. When people get greedy, they throw caution to the wind and proceed without thinking. Sometimes greed is the very factor that the con artists count on. Some people think they can get away with anything, and they walk away with nothing. A perfect example is the unscrupulous fellow who attempted to use his minority status as a ticket to free rent for himself and several undocumented immigrants. Here's the story.

A landlord had a tenant who used his residence as a "home base" for almost twenty people, all of whom were in this country in violation of immigration policy. The landlord wanted these people out, but the tenant threatened to portray his landlord as a xenophobe, prejudiced against immigrant minorities. Believing he held the upper hand by threat, the tenant had not paid a cent in rent for a solid year.

Not wanting this false and damaging publicity, the landlord finally hired me to take care of the situation. Promising that I would get this undesirable pack of cohorts off his property, I went to the home in disguise and claimed to represent a major real estate developer who owned an exclusive residential high-rise in Century City.

I told the tenant that the developer was in serious trouble with the Department of Fair Housing for not renting to minorities, and was about to be hit with a substantial fine.

"The developer is offering free rent for a year," I lied, "if you will move in immediately." The tenant was understandably disbelieving, so I took him to a five-million-dollar penthouse and let him have a look around.

Needless to say, the tenant was rather impressed. He agreed to move in under three conditions: he wanted the keys to the condo immediately, an electronic key to the underground garage, and sixty dollars for moving expenses.

I agreed to all three conditions and gave the man sixty dollars. The greedy tenant couldn't believe his luck. He immediately packed the truck with his belongings, loaded up eighteen of his friends, and headed off to his new home in Century City.

When he arrived, he found his luck had changed. The doorman had never heard of the real estate developer, the keys didn't fit the lock, and the electronic key for the underground garage was an expired Shell credit card that had been painted black.

Heading back to his old home didn't help either. Armed guards were now stationed outside, and the locks had been changed. According to California law, once the premises are vacated, all renter's rights are relinquished.

I kept my promise to the landlord—his greedy tenant was gone, as was the threat of slander and libel. Yes, it all starts and ends with greed.

A client whose friends were taken by a conman to the tune of eight million dollars contacted me. It was a typical con. He approached his marks by offering them twenty or thirty percent on their money in a very short time. With his first victims, the conman invested fifty thousand dollars of theirs in a motion picture deal. Within two months, he returned seventy-eight thousand dollars, a profit of twenty-eight thousand dollars. His first victims were thrilled, returned the check for seventy-eight thousand dollars, and asked if it could be reinvested.

The conman agreed to invest the money in the next deal coming up in a couple of weeks, but he had to hold on to the money, as he would need it at a moment's notice. They agreed to let him hold the money. They received the check for seventy-eight thousand dollars but never cashed it. In truth, that check would have bounced: the account only had four thousand dollars in it at the time.

The victims couldn't wait to get their friends involved. They told all their wealthy pals about their new investment counselor. They extolled virtues by showing their friends a copy of his bogus check. It soon snowballed. Everyone was calling the conman to invest, and the returns were great. Only one person pulled out early after investing one hundred thousand dollars. He received a check for one hundred sixty-nine thousand dollars.

In only three months, the conman had a bankroll and was wheeling and dealing. He actually turned down some people he didn't like; their investment was too small. He was now only dealing with people who would be willing to invest at least one hundred thousand dollars. This went on for about eighteen months until the conman had accumulated over eight million dollars. This was safely put away overseas in numerous motion picture deals, or so they all thought. To add credibility to his operation, he rented a large swanky office and furniture to match. It was an impressive operation. But it was all a façade.

The problem with investing with conmen is that the return on your investment is limited to the length of time he continues to operate. Once he has accumulated his money, the deal somehow falls apart. The crook suddenly either has a problem with the company he invested in overseas or the overseas market has fallen—neither of which, he sadly laments, he has any control over.

My client and his friends hired me to find any assets so that they could recoup at least some of their money. My contract said that I would receive twenty-five percent of all monies found, plus a three-thousand-dollar retainer to cover expenses. The client would also have forty-eight hours from the time I found the assets to tie them up, or to execute on their judgment. After forty-eight hours, if they did not get the money, they still owed me my fee. In the interim, they must place half of the money owed to me in a bank trust account. That money would be released to me after verification of the assets. I then obtained a lien on the second half of the money, so I am first paid. They agreed to my terms and conditions, and signed the contract.

After five months of tracking the money, I found three million of eight million dollars. He had a very elaborate scheme: He had deposited the money in a local bank. Then he would transfer the money to a bogus motion picture company in Italy. A second investment company in France invoiced the Italian company for services rendered. The money was transferred to France, where it was then transferred via wire to a third company in England.

A company in New York owned by the conman's brother and mother would then invoice the English company. They would in turn invest the money in CDs, stocks, bonds, and real property under a corporate name. It was the best-planned and thought-out scheme I had ever encountered. The total assets of their investments, minus their living expenses, were substantial. I had found two million dollars in liquid assets and the rest tied up in worldwide investments.

I contacted my client, telling him that I was able to locate three million in assets, and requested that he place half my fee in trust. He wanted to know where the assets were before he would deposit the money. I explained to him that this was not the deal. I would divulge the fruits of my five-month investigation only after he deposited the money. He begged and pleaded with me to tell him the location of the assets.

After two weeks, it was obvious that he had no intention of living up to his end of the agreement. He contacted his lawyer, who was also a victim of the con, who tried to intimidate me into revealing the whereabouts of the conman's assets.

I realized that any further involvement with these greedy people would be fruitless. To buy myself time, I gave them worthless information that was in direct proportion to what they had paid me for my five months' work. But it bought me enough time to sell the information to the IRS, who would guarantee me in writing ten percent of all taxes collected by them. Since the total worth of the income that they had received was twelve million dollars, the tax liability would be about six million, plus interest and penalties that had accrued on the money for the last four years.

I estimated my ten percent was worth in the neighborhood of about nine hundred thousand dollars and was backed by the treasury of the US government. After my client couldn't find the money, they asked for a refund of the money they advanced me for expenses. I gladly returned their three thousand dollars and cashed a check from Uncle Sam for close to one million dollars. Greed doesn't pay.

One look at showbusiness lawsuits reveals that having a hit TV series or a price tag of twenty million dollars per film will not protect you from a cheating spouse, a burgled house, or a "good friend" swindling you out of your hard-earned cash.

Average folks sit and watch their clothes at public laundromats because if they don't keep an eye on their belongings, someone will steal their jeans and T-shirts. The rich and famous do not sit at laundromats, but the same concern prevails.

The Rolling Stones' guitarist Ron Woods had his jeans stolen—jeans studded with diamonds. His response, of course, was not to simply say, "Darn it, I should have kept an eye on them." Instead, he hired me to find the impressive, if impractical, Levi's and get them back. I did.

Of course, I am a real private detective. Not only that, but I've played one in the movies—Raymond Chandler's Phillip Marlowe in the private eye classic *Chandler Creates Marlowe*. You don't have to be a real private detective to act like Phillip Marlowe, Sam Spade, Jim Rockford, or Mike Hammer, and you don't need to learn from tragic mistakes before you "wise up."

Sad but true, even I had to wise up. I was famous for protecting others, but I left myself vulnerable. If I had hired me to protect me, I wouldn't have been poisoned, drugged, and robbed of over sixteen million dollars.

Of course, when the poison was out of my system and the drugs wore off, I promptly hired myself to get it back.

You are about to learn how to stop dishonest people from hurting you—be they so-called friends or loyal employees. I will show you how to know for sure if your lover or spouse is cheating on you, or if you are getting involved with someone who is hiding something.

Using the secrets I've used for years as a Hollywood private detective, you will increase your odds of finding missing persons, runaway kids, or stolen clothing. If you want to:

- track down money that has been stolen from you

- find and secure assets that your spouse is trying to hide in a divorce case
- prevent others from finding out things about you that you don't want them to know.

All you must do is keep reading, and put what you learn to work for you. I promise you; it is all here in *Secrets of a Hollywood Private Eye.*

—Fred Wolfson, PI

CHAPTER ONE

CHEATING SPOUSES

There is an old Arab proverb, "When a man gets an erection, he loses seventy-five percent of his religion." That may be an understatement. Often, the man loses one hundred percent of his marriage and fifty percent of his assets.

Men can't have an affair alone, and married women are almost equally unfaithful. The Hite Report on Male Sexuality (1981) found that seventy-two percent of men married two years or more had had an extramarital affair; the Hite survey of women (1976) found that seventy percent of women married five years or more had had an extramarital affair.

Sadly, having an affair can become a behavior pattern for both sexes. According to recent research, approximately fifteen percent of women and twenty-five percent of men have more than four affairs during their married lives.

You may already be familiar with the ten telltale signs of cheating. If you are not aware of them, you should be.

1. He claims he is working late and then doesn't pick up the phone.
2. You check the car odometer after she has driven to and from work, knowing the mileage is fourteen miles... and she is, on some nights, putting on sixty-four miles.

3. You go through her phonebook and find names and phone numbers in code.
4. You go through his phonebook and find numbers that appear on your phone bill. You run those numbers through the phone company to find out Carl Cummings is really Carol Johnson.
5. You run a marriage check on him through the local state and find three marriages and one divorce you didn't know about.
6. You go through her purse or wallet and find names and phone numbers hidden away in a secret compartment.
7. You find women's panties in the glovebox of the car, and you don't have a teenage son who borrows the car.
8. You go through the credit card bills and find restaurant charges on nights he was working. You call the restaurant and find out from the receipt number that it was dinner for two.
9. You go through her checkbook and find checks for clothing for the opposite sex that you never received. Around Christmas and birthdays, you should wait for the occasion to pass before the confrontation.
10. He has condoms; you are on the pill.

There are other so-called danger signals. Beware, all of these can have innocent explanations.
1. He suddenly starts losing weight, wearing different cologne, and changes his hairstyle.
2. She closes down your joint bank account and opens a new one in her name only.
3. He cancels his life insurance policy.
4. After years of being affectionate, he tells you that you are smothering him.
5. Your sex life appears on the endangered species list.
6. Her sexual technique changes dramatically.

7. He asks you to do things sexually he never asked for previously.
8. She calls out someone else's name during a climax.
9. Your friends tell you that they saw your loved one with someone else in a restaurant holding hands.
10. He claims he must go on a business trip and won't tell you where he is going.
11. She tells you she is leaving on a business trip to Cleveland on United Airlines, but no such reservation exists.
12. When she returns from a business trip, you find a hotel receipt under the names of a Mr. and Mrs.
13. He joins a social club with meetings every Thursday night. His car, however, is never in the parking lot of the social club on Thursday nights.
14. She joins a bowling league and you can never find her in those alleys.

Yes, those all seem suspicious. Before you embarrass yourself with false accusations, make sure you are not projecting your own insecurities or personal guilt. Allow me to give you a few illuminating examples from my own files.

Back before American travelers experienced Soviet Union-style restrictions, a clothing store chain hired a Washington state television director to shoot some commercials in Hawaii. Part of the deal included the use of his favorite cinematographer and one attractive female model with whom he previously worked.

To save money, the client took advantage of a "family fare" promotion with the airlines and booked all three under the director's last name. This was also done at the hotel, where the three were given a suite under his name. The model actually had her own hotel room, although it was located inside the suite. The two men shared #410; the woman was in #410-A.

The director, unaware of the hotel reservation peculiarities until his arrival, gave his wife the hotel phone number before leaving town. She estimated the time of his arrival and called the hotel.

When she asked if her husband was registered there, she was informed, "Yes, the three of them checked in to suite 410 just a few minutes ago."

The wife, assuming the worst, accused her husband and the cameraman of having a wild tryst with the young lady. No amount of reassurance from the cameraman, the model, or the client would convince her otherwise. Her erroneous conclusion-jumping did not help their marriage, and her continual accusatory phone calls to all concerned disrupted the project and damaged the creative atmosphere.

"Not only that," recalled the director, "but this was in August, and it was hotter than hell. We were working long, tedious hours. I think we had one afternoon to ourselves, during which I stewed over my home situation while the woman I was supposedly having the affair with was gift shopping for her real-life lover and kids back home. The idea of having an affair hadn't occurred to me at all—by the end of the trip, it was sounding more and more like something I could easily justify if the opportunity dropped in my lap."

Indeed, the business traveler, male or female, is most vulnerable to an extramarital affair. Anyone who travels extensively as part of their employment knows that the glamour and fun of traveling is short-lived when it is a constant occurrence. Baggage claim becomes a nightmare, flight attendants appear hostile, and fellow passengers seem agents of fate sent to repay you for every bad deed in your life. You land at airports in the middle of summer that have lost their air conditioning; you land at airports not on your itinerary because of weather conditions in winter. Hotels give you the wrong keys for the right room, or the right keys for the wrong room. Outside your window is a vehicle whose car alarm wails incessantly; you hear sexual participants in the next room going for the gold in the erotic Olympics.

From tardy room service to rental cars with faulty ignitions, business travel can be one stressful event after another, especially when it is part of your life on a regular basis. Consider the following true-life example, an example that is a perfect set-up for an affair.

You are on a multi-city business trip. It is winter in Denver, ice and snow. Some freeway off-ramps are closed. After dropping off your rental car, you have to hustle like hell to make the flight. You can make it if you run, and pray you are not "randomly selected" at security for a full body search and in-depth investigation.

You make it just in time to experience one of these two dispiriting events: your plane pulling back from the gate, or the flight is canceled. You sleep in the airport, waiting for the next flight out. After several hours, you feel like a POW.

Then she (or he) catches your eye. This person is in the same situation and shares your destination. What happens next is a perfectly natural phenomenon investigated by scientists as far back as the 1960s. A person under emotional stress will immediately bond with, and be sexually attracted to, the first decent-looking person of the opposite sex they talk to. It has something to do with the survival of the species.

In some primitive part of the human brain, stress is associated with threat to life. Threat to life sends a signal to propagate the species—in other words, SEX.

None of the above-mentioned process is conscious. From the business traveler's perspective, travel just became more pleasurable because of attractive company: a companion who, like you, will gladly exchange pulling out their hair in dismay for clawing the sheets in delight.

You don't even notice the flight since you are in a first-date mode—charming, talkative, and very important.

Life's little problems fade away. The flight attendants seem pleasant again. The food is a good excuse to have dinner with your new traveling partner. When you arrive at your destination, you find out where your new friend is staying, and make plans to meet later that evening for a drink, maybe dinner.

The evening turns out great. You return to your room, date in hand, and spend the next three days missing meetings at the convention you were scheduled to attend. The person in the next room goes home talking about the sexual Olympics that occurred all night in the adjoining room.

So it starts: the beginning of the end of the relationship that you developed back home. It wasn't planned, it "just happened."

Most first affairs are cases of accidental infidelity, unplanned acts completely out of character with the person's self-image. "The most startling dynamic behind accidental infidelity," says noted expert Frank Pittman, "is misplaced politeness, the feeling that it would be rude to turn down a needy friend's sexual advances. In the debonair gallantry of the moment, the brazen discourtesy to the marriage partner is overlooked altogether."

Once someone has an affair, he or she makes one of four decisions.

1. Decide that it was a stupid thing to do, and resolve not to do it again.
2. Decide that the infidelity is because your spouse let you down, and then go home and make your marriage fail.
3. Decide that this is a new, fun, and inexpensive hobby.
4. Decide you must be married to the wrong person, and declare your love to your new bed partner.

All but the first are tragic errors of judgment. Fewer than ten percent of people having affairs divorce their spouse and marry their lover. Seventy-five percent of these marriages end in divorce.

In most crimes, be they legal crimes or crimes of the heart, the perpetrator does not want to suffer the humiliation accompanying the revelation of impropriety, but fear of punishment is the world's worst motivator.

No man, or woman, lives happily ever after in a fear-based relationship. In fact, as our television commercial director noted, the continual assumption that he was cheating provided possible justification for doing exactly that should the opportunity arise.

The vice president of one of the big three television networks contacted us. "My wife is having an affair," he insisted. "I've hired three other firms to catch her, but they have all failed."

The reason they failed was simple: she would always look in her rear-view mirror and if she suspected that she was being followed, she would not show up for her rendezvous. This went on for about three days. We told our client the only way to tail his wife would be by helicopter, but it would be quite costly. He said that money wasn't an issue. He had to know.

We rented a helicopter from a local airport at a cost of two hundred dollars per hour. The helicopter served as a command post that coordinated the activities of four investigators in rental cars on the ground.

We started tracking her when she left her place of employment at about 11:30 a.m. She drove around Westwood for about thirty minutes before entering a local hotel. Our ground units were in hot pursuit. She didn't check in, but went right to the elevator with a female operative following. She knocked on door 532 and was let in by a man wearing a bathrobe.

Our operative contacted the helicopter via radio, and the message was relayed to our client via cellular telephone. He was about fifteen minutes away; he drove over and waited by her car in the below-ground garage, hidden about three cars away. Within the hour, the post-coital couple walked over to her car, embraced, and kissed passionately.

As you may imagine, our client was displeased with his wife's behavior, and even more irked at the actions of her paramour. In fact, he punched her lover in the mouth, broke some teeth, and more punching and hitting continued until the police arrived.

Our client was first charged with battery, but the case was dismissed as mutual combat. His cheating wife moved to Cleveland the same day. He filed for divorce. It was uncontested. He was a rich television executive; the lover (no, he didn't go to Cleveland with the wife) had nothing special to offer except infidelity. Being rich and semi-famous did not protect my television executive client from heartbreak and deception.

I've been hired by famous people, worked with them on television and in motion pictures, and I've also investigated famous people. Some of them are wacky as rabbits; others are emotionally insecure individuals who pay a high price for high income and front-page fame. A perfect example is the peculiar romantic coupling of comic Roseanne Barr with comedy writer/actor Tom Arnold.

Tom Arnold, despite his personal peculiarities—or perhaps because of them—is an incredible talent. That does not mean his particular talent is obvious to everyone or appeals to me personally. As a writer, producer, and actor, Arnold has established himself with both television and film audiences worldwide, having won such awards as the Peabody Award for writing and a Golden Globe for writing and producing.

His introduction to Hollywood began after he moved to Los Angeles as a writer on the first run of the highly successful television series *Roseanne* before eventually serving as executive producer of the sitcom. Of course, he married the show's star, Roseanne Barr, and that is where I come into the story.

Before they were married, Arnold wrote intimate love letters to Barr. Somehow, this highly personal correspondence wound up published in the *National Enquirer*. "Someone stole these letters," said Arnold, "and obviously sold them for a hell of a lot of money. I want you to find the love letters, and find out who sold them to the *National Enquirer*."

I have worked for the *National Enquirer*. They were a little slow in paying but have a high degree of integrity compared to other tabloids. Before they publish any story about a major celebrity, they do extensive fact checking, and actually require independent sources to verify virtually every detail.

Most people think that celebrity stories come from some secondary source, such as a talkative house cleaner or a bought-off limo driver. The majority of the stories actually come from the celebrities themselves or their publicists.

In Hollywood, the old adage, "there is no bad publicity as long as they spell your name right" still applies. If a publicist goes to the *LA Times* and tells them that their client's marriage is on the rocks, the chances of that story ever seeing publication are remote. The publicist's choices are limited because most of the time, there is nothing happening in a celebrity's life that is very newsworthy. So, they do the next best thing; they run to the *National Enquirer*, planting a story that gets their client's name in front of readers.

The relationship between your favorite stars and the *National Enquirer* is very much one of love-hate. The stars say they hate the *Enquirer*, yet when things are slow, they use the *Enquirer* and in return, the *Enquirer* uses them to sell to their dedicated readers.

The cases I worked on for the *Enquirer* involved verifying stories about celebrities prior to publication. I knew most of the reporters in the L.A. office and the editors back in Lantana, Florida. All of them were very nice to me. The only reason I stopped working for them was that my price became too high; I left on good terms and we were still friendly.

When fellow private detective Bob Frasco approached me on the Roseanne Barr love letters case, I had severed my relationship with the *Enquirer* so there was no conflict of interest.

The first thing Bob wanted was a polygraph test of all the employees working in the Arnold/Barr residence. Most likely, the purloined letter caper was an inside job.

Barr and Arnold lived in a thirty-five hundred square foot home in Beverly Hills. The "office" was formerly the garage, converted for business purposes.

I showed up with a secretary/assistant from the Frasco Agency. Tom Arnold, clad only in boxer shorts and flip-flops, met us at the door. The head of his flaccid penis peeked out of his shorts. I was a bit taken aback; the woman averted her eyes.

After an equally short introduction, Arnold said, "I'm not taking that test. You know that, don't you?"

"You're the client, Tom," I replied. "I'll test whomever you want tested."

"I don't like the whole testing idea but it's something that has to be done, just not to me."

He introduced me to his executive assistant, a young fellow named Chris. The two men met at a photo store where Chris was an employee. Eager to work for a star, Chris' persistence in pursuing his goal convinced Arnold to bring the fellow on board as his own form of personal security.

Chris was the first employee I selected for polygraph testing, and the first person subjected to an in-depth interview. Some people with certain medical histories are exempt, as results can be inaccurate. Then again, polygraph results are, in the final analysis, unreliable in general.

I also wanted to find out as much as possible about his involvement in the case. During the interview, Chris offered me his telephone bills for the previous three months. "I can prove I didn't make any calls to the *Enquirer*," he said. "I'll even show you my bank statements. The only money I've deposited is my paycheck."

"Wonderful, Chris," I responded. "In fact, I'll drive you home right now and we can get that stuff."

As we were leaving, Arnold asked us where we were going. I told him that Chris was willing to produce his phone records and bank statements.

"Okay," said Tom with a scowl. "Get right back. I have other things to do besides test people all day. I have a company to run and a show to get out." As we were leaving, Roseanne came out of her bedroom and headed for her Jeep. Chris and I said hello to her, and we took off.

Chris lived with his girlfriend in an apartment in the Valley. We arrived at the apartment and started looking through the records. The phone rang. It was Arnold.

"I don't like you getting so personal," he said. "Looking through Chris' records and stuff."

"Well, I assure you, Mr. Arnold," I told him evenly, "that Chris volunteered to show me the records, and he hasn't been coerced in any way." That seemed to settle it.

Not more than two minutes later, the phone rang again. Chris handed me the phone. "It's Roseanne," he said.

"Yes, may I help you?"

"This is Roseanne Barr," she barked, "and I want this whole investigation to stop. I want you to leave Chris alone right now. We love him and trust him and I do not want him going through this. Do you understand me?"

"You are the client," I told her, "and I'll respect your wishes." As I did with her husband, I assured her of Chris' voluntary cooperation.

"I don't care," she said emphatically. "I want this thing to stop right now. I have had enough of this. Take him home, and leave us alone. Do you understand me?"

"Yes, I understand you."

I drove back to Roseanne's home, dropped off Chris, packed my polygraph, and my assistant and I left the house. On the way back to the office, my assistant told me that while Chris and I were gone, Tom Arnold paced back and forth like a caged lion.

"The entire time you were gone," she told me, "he kept harping at me, saying stuff such as, 'Is this what I'm paying you for, to just sit around?' I explained that he wasn't getting charged anything extra for my time. He seemed very uptight. What's his problem?"

"He's got a lot on his mind, probably," I answered, figuring it is always easier to excuse than accuse. "I'm sure famous people in his position are under more pressure than an astronaut."

In truth, it was a wasted day. Nothing accomplished. Roseanne and Tom hired us, yet both blocked the most basic aspects of the investigation. Investigator Bob Frasco and I decided to take another approach—instead of finding out who sold the letters, we would find out from whom the *Enquirer* bought them. Different question; same answer. Our new approach: penetrate the *Enquirer*.

STEP ONE: THE DIVERSION

I contacted an honest, ethical *Enquirer* reporter named Lyita Enisastas, and made her an offer I knew she would refuse. "Lyita," I said in conspiratorial tones, "I'll give you five thousand dollars if you reveal your source on the Roseanne Barr story."

She went ballistic. "I wouldn't sell a source for a million dollars," she insisted angrily. "I can't believe that you would even ask me to do such a thing." She then hung up on me and immediately contacted corporate headquarters, informing them of my unethical offer. This was exactly what I wanted.

I then contacted *Enquirer* assistant editor John South, another loyal employee. "John, I'm in tight with Roseanne Barr," I lied. "I'll give you exclusive stories about Roseanne for the next year if you'll reveal your source on the love letters." He denied my request, as did the *Enquirer*'s president, Ian Calder. This was perfect. The *Enquirer* now felt one hundred percent secure that I would *not* be getting information about the love letters from them. As I had gone all the way to the top with an offer to buy the information and been refused, the matter was settled. The *National Enquirer* felt secure that I would not obtain the information; the matter was closed. Their image of me as an ethical reporter was certainly damaged, but that could be repaired when the truth came out.

STEP TWO: THE CON

Because the *Enquirer* was notoriously a slow paying organization, I was on first-name basis with the much-harassed folks in accounts payable. I called in, disguised my voice, and pretended I was a reporter from their Los Angeles office.

"Hey, I need your help," I said. "One of my sources insists they didn't get paid for a story, and I'm sure they did. Please pull the Roseanne file and read off the names of all the sources that we paid on Roseanne Barr stories." She pulled the file, giving me the names, the amounts, the check numbers, the dates of the checks, the banks on which they were drawn, and the reference number of each story, and where the checks were mailed.

"Do me one more quick favor," I asked politely, "just fax me a copy of the front and back of the cleared checks." I gave her the number of a fax machine at Quick Copy print shop on the other side of the city.

Next, I sent one of my people, dressed as a messenger, to pick up the fax. Even hotshot private eyes make mistakes, and here's where I made mine: I neglected informing Quick Copy of the incoming fax and that a messenger was on his way to pick it up under my assumed name.

The print shop was not expecting anything from the *National Enquirer*, so they called and asked for whom they should hold the fax. The *National Enquirer* ordered them not to release the fax. The *Enquirer* would send an employee, with credentials, to get the documents. If Quick Copy released that fax to anyone else, the *Enquirer* would sue.

Not knowing any of this at the time, I called Quick Copy under my assumed name and asked if I received anything from the *National Enquirer*. The next thing I knew, Quick Copy's manager was reading me the riot act, not the fax information. I was semi-screwed: I had all the information, but not that hardcopy proof that would crack the case.

I had every name of every person who sold a Roseanne story to the *Enquirer*. Reading over the list, my attitude towards Roseanne Barr softened considerably. Selling chunks of her private life were many of her so-called trusted friends and confidants. People she had treated as family used her as nothing more than an exploitable cash cow.

One of the checks was payable only to a social security number as added secrecy. The one story meriting that degree of secrecy was the love letters. Once I researched the social security number, I knew who sold Tom Arnold's love letters to the *National Enquirer*. It was Tom Arnold.

Here, apparently, is what happened. Tom Arnold and Roseanne Barr were engaged to be married, but he had a drug problem that Roseanne wouldn't tolerate. She called it off, telling him he had to choose between his "domestic goddess" (Roseanne) and his "white lady" (cocaine).

Tom, resentful, sold the love letters to the *National Enquirer*. Roseanne took Tom back; they were married in January. The letters hit the newsstand in February. There was no way for Tom to save face. He continued his charade all the way through, making a false police report to the LAPD and the FBI, and then going along with the federal litigation against the *Enquirer*.

I gave my report to Bob Frasco, and he gave the report to Roseanne and Tom. They paid the bill in full. The litigation, of course, came to an abrupt halt.

The Tom Arnold/Roseanne Barr relationship was not destined to be the great love story of the twentieth century. Their union, sadly doomed, ended in divorce. Sometimes it is hard to tell the victims from the perpetrators.

I am sure it broke Roseanne's heart to discover that Tom sold the letters. It was painful enough to learn how many of her so-called close friends and co-workers sold pieces of her life to the tabloids. To them, she wasn't a real person, she was an exploitable oddity.

At least Tom Arnold didn't try to kill her, drive her insane, or turn her into a drooling incompetent so he could gain control of her fortune. That is exactly what I believe Erin Fleming attempted against famed comic Groucho Marx.

Fleming appeared in minor roles in five films from 1965 through 1976, during which time she became acquainted with Groucho Marx and became his secretary, assistant, promoter, cheerleader, and perhaps his number one exploiter.

Her influence on Groucho was controversial, with Groucho's son, Arthur Marx, describing her in Svengaliesque terms. In the years leading up to Groucho's death in 1977, his heirs filed several lawsuits against her.

Groucho was, in his later years, a pathetic figure unable to care for himself or act in his own best interests. Erin Fleming hired me to protect Groucho from alleged attempts on his life. Fleming claimed that Groucho's son, Arthur, was trying to kill his father in eagerness to inherit Groucho's millions.

It was no secret that Groucho wasn't Arthur's nominee for Father of the Year, and Fleming was credited with getting Groucho his recent special recognition at the Academy Awards and revitalizing interest in all things involving the famed Marx Brothers. I considered it an honor to have Erin Fleming as a client and to be of service to Groucho Marx.

Arthur Marx and Erin Fleming were disputants in an upcoming hearing regarding the conservatorship of Groucho and his assets. Since the conservatorship hearing was less than a week away, she claimed that in case there was an attempt on his life, she wanted a reliable witness who could come forward and testify on her behalf.

As she was the client, I took her at her word and assigned two armed off-duty police officers to the residence. The first day they both quit, claiming they didn't want any part of this woman—she was, they claimed, "the bitch from hell."

I immediately hired new men, but their response was the same. Every time I hired agents to work at Groucho's house, they would resign that same day. Obviously, this case demanded my on-scene personal attention.

I arrived at the house at 8 a.m. on a Tuesday, just as my last shift was walking off the job, claiming that they didn't need money that badly. Located on Hillcrest Drive in Trousdale Estate next to Beverly Hills, it was a large house filled with old memories. There were pictures of Groucho with every big celebrity in Hollywood on all of the walls. I am not easily impressed, but this was impressive. This was the home of a showbusiness legend.

I wasn't in the house for five minutes when I heard loud screaming coming from the back bedroom. Following the insults to their source, I found Erin standing over Groucho, yelling, "Sign the check. Sign the check, you fucking old bastard. Sign the fucking check."

"Excuse me," I interjected, "what exactly is going on here?"

Erin, outraged at my presence, replied angrily, "As far as you're concerned, I am Mrs. Groucho Marx, do you understand? What's going on here is none of your damn business."

I bit my tongue, nodded, and left the room. Insulted and pissed off, I decided to walk outside and check the perimeter. Perhaps the fresh air would help me calm down.

As I walked past the storm drain in front of the house, something unusual caught my attention—a brown paper bag stuffed in the drain. Kneeling down, I reached in and pulled the bag out onto the lawn. Inside the bag were used syringes and medication with Groucho Marx's name it.

I brought the bag back into the house and asked a nurse if Groucho was receiving any type of injectables. The nurse said that Groucho was a diabetic and they were injecting him with insulin. I asked about the yellow capsules and the nurse claimed she had never seen them before. I took one of the capsules and a syringe and placed them in my car.

I confronted Erin with my discovery. She said that Groucho had suffered a stroke and was under medication by his doctor. I asked what the doctor had prescribed and she claimed that she didn't know specifically what the doctor prescribed, but whatever it was, it was none of my business.

I asked her about the yellow capsules that I had found in the storm drain. She said that they were placebos. She said Groucho had become addicted to some medication and that the doctor had prescribed placebos until he could be weaned off the medication. I asked her why the "placebos" had a number written on the side. Most placebos I have seen don't have any identifying marks. She had no explanation for the yellow pills. She said, "Give them to me and I'll take care of them." She then asked me where I had found them. I told her I found them in the storm drain. She didn't believe me and told me to leave her alone.

That night, I took the syringes, pills, and other medications to an independent lab to have them analyzed. The chemist found the yellow pills contained a barbiturate. The syringes also contained traces of the same barbiturate, as did the injectable solution.

The next day, I asked the private duty nurse if Groucho was on any type of barbiturate. She claimed that he wasn't. I asked how the trace elements of barbiturates got into the solution they were injecting every day. She had no explanation.

That same day, much to my surprise, I was invited to join Groucho and Erin for lunch. Groucho was at the head of the table, Erin was at his left side, and I was sitting at his right side. The family cook served the meal, and did so as if absolutely terrified of Fleming. I soon understood the reason for her fearful demeanor.

Since Groucho had a stroke, he had lost some control of his muscular system. He had trouble eating, and sometimes, he would miss his mouth completely. When this happened, Erin yelled, "Groucho, you fucking pig. Don't drop your food like a dog or I will make you eat off the floor like a dog."

Once again, Groucho started to drool and miss his mouth. Erin took his plate, threw it on the floor, and yelled at the top of her lungs, "You stupid fucking dog. Eat off the floor like a stupid dog should, you old fucking dog!"

I could not sit there and pretend such rude, abusive behavior was tolerable. I had to say something. "He is an old man with physical problems; there is no reason to treat him so rudely."

"Why the fuck is anything that goes on in this house any of your business," she snapped. "Where the fuck do you get off questioning anything I do? Don't you realize who I am? I am Mrs. Groucho Marx and you are a fucking idiot who I don't want in my house. Now get the fuck out of here before I kill you or have you killed."

Obviously, I needn't save room for dessert.

"Do you understand how dangerous someone like me can be?" she ranted. "Do you? Do you? I could have you killed by the time I snap my fingers, as I could have anyone killed who crosses me. Killed now. You understand who I am, don't you?"

I politely set aside my cutlery before responding, lest inadvertent gesturing be mistaken for assault with a culinary weapon. "No, I really don't," I responded evenly. "All that I can see is an old man being abused by some angry, manipulative, gold-digging has-been actress who will pay for what she has done, either in a court of law or in hell."

I got up from the table and walked out the door. She was still threatening to have me killed when I closed the door behind me. She hired me to protect Groucho and that was exactly what I was going to do.

I made an appointment with Detective Brooks of the Beverly Hills Police Department, and showed him the evidence found in the storm drain. I also advised him of the abusive behavior.

Next, I consulted my attorney to see how I could prevent this crazed woman from getting conservatorship of Groucho. He instructed me to attend the upcoming conservatorship hearing as *amicus curiae*—a friend of the court.

Launching a full-scale investigation at my own expense, I found nurses formerly employed in the Marx home whose testimony verified and validated my allegations of abuse. In the investigative process, I also found a cook, living in Canada, whom Erin had allegedly offered ten thousand dollars to poison Groucho.

The first day of the trial was a three-ring circus. Erin Fleming walked into court believing her claim was uncontested. Groucho's son, Arthur, had given up; she knew of no legal reason why she should not become Groucho's conservator. Then I showed up.

It became a madhouse of surprises, allegations, and reporters clamoring for interviews. Erin Fleming went ballistic. Before I could get home that night, Erin was banging on my front door. My fiancée called the police, and I arrived about the same time as the cops.

Erin was with a group of people yelling and screaming outside my home. They were chanting and yelling death threats to everyone who came in their path. As the police arrived, she yelled to them to watch out, saying I had a gun.

The police drew their service revolvers and instructed me to interlock my fingers behind my head and not to move. One of the officers patted me down as the other pointed his gun at me. The officer who was patting me down asked me where the gun was. I told him that I didn't have a gun but to go ahead and check for himself. When he didn't find any gun, he asked Erin where she had seen one. She replied that I always carry a gun.

The focus of their attention switched to her. They asked who lived here and I replied that I did. They asked Erin what she was doing there with her group of friends yelling and chanting.

She told them a story of how I had gone into court and perjured myself by lying about her, and that she wanted me arrested for perjury.

The police officers instructed the group to disperse and to stay away from my house and me. As she walked away, she yelled, "Death to the pigs!" They both looked at me in disgust and told me if she came back to call them and they would arrest her for disturbing the peace.

That night, the phone calls started. At first, they would just call and hang up. But as it got later, the calls became more aggressive. They started telling me that Manson had nothing on them and that I would pay for what I had done. Then they came out with actual death threats. They told me that I would be killed when I least expected it. I took the phone off the hook and waited for anything else that might occur. I knew this woman was crazy. But just how crazy, I had no idea. The trial went on for a long time.

Erin lost the conservatorship battle and so did Arthur. It was given to an old-time friend of the family, Nat Perrin. Groucho lived for three more years.

I don't dispute any good things Fleming may have done for Groucho early on. I wasn't there to see it, so I won't contradict it. I do know what I saw, what I heard, and I would not keep silent.

After Groucho's death, Bank of America sued Fleming for $472,000, claiming she coerced him to give her money and gifts above and beyond her earned salary as his secretary. She didn't have the money. "All I have in my checking account is thirty dollars," said Fleming. She passed away on April 15, 2003.

People asked me for an exclusive interview, giving them the in-depth story on what went on inside the Marx home. According to the reporter, I was the true centerpiece of the story. I gently refused their kind offer, content that simple, accurate reporting would sufficiently portray the depth of my involvement.

One week later, I was discontent; *People*'s story on the Marx fracas, despite acknowledging the important testimony of the nurses and caregivers I brought forward, left me out of the story altogether.

People, in a dazzling display of insufficient fact checking, reported that Erin hired two private detectives to find out if Arthur Marx was bugging his father's house. The two gumshoes allegedly turned against her, claiming she threatened to kill them, and were "now trying to peddle paperback rights to their story."

Disgusted with the distortion of truth, and appalled by the now proven disingenuous pitch of *People*'s reporter, I promptly cancelled my subscription. I'm sure they are still reeling from the shock of this sudden financial embargo.

Arthur Marx graciously expressed his gratitude, and assured me that he would send enough work my way to make up for whatever this altruistic act cost me in time and lost fees. "Expect my call, Fred," said Arthur. That was 1977. It was nice of him to say, although I did not really expect his call then, and I certainly do not expect it now.

Expectations, be they good or bad, are often the undoing of both the cheater and the cheated. Consider the story of multi-millionaire real-estate tycoon, Harry, and beautiful movie actress, Sally.

Harry, one of the most eligible wealthy bachelors in Beverly Hills, attended an exclusive black-tie event—the fiftieth birthday party of a Hollywood mogul. Harry arrived at the party about 8 p.m. and soon after met Sally, a lovely twenty-eight-year-old up-and-coming actress. Sally was bright, charming, and well dressed. He found no fault with her, but the attraction did not seem mutual. He tried all night to form some sort of conversational bond, but one diversion or another interrupted every attempt.

By night's end, Harry was almost obsessed. Finally, as she was leaving the event, he wrote down her license plate number. The next day, Harry called his attorney and inquired as to the best way of finding Sally's home address and phone number. The attorney contacted our firm, and by the next day, we had Sally's personal information. We were not going to hand it over, of course, without making sure Harry wasn't some psychotic stalker.

Our requirements for obtaining this information are quite strict. We must have a working relationship with the attorney and we must know the client and his intentions to avoid obsessed fans.

Harry was pleased with our findings and started sending Sally large baskets of exotic and beautiful flowers. Enclosed in basket was a card from Harry. The first one read, "I hope you don't find this too forward, but we met at a party last night and I would really like to spend some more time with you." Harry provided his name and number. The flowers were in her vestibule, and the ball was in her court.

Two weeks went by with no reply. Finally, Harry got up the nerve to call Sally. When the phone rang, a woman with a foreign accent answered it. Harry asked for Sally. The voice on the other end explained that Sally had been out of the country for the last two weeks, but was expected back that evening. Harry asked if she had received the flowers, and the voice assured him of daily delivery.

Returning home, Sally encountered a remarkable display of half-dead flowers. She asked her secretary what was happening, and after listening to the story, Sally called Harry. She thanked him profusely, and explained that she had been working on a motion picture for the last two weeks. They got along famously in the phone, and made a lunch date for the following afternoon.

From that lunch forward, it was a whirlwind courtship—romantic trips to Paris and cruising aboard private yachts in the Mediterranean. Three months later, Harry asked Sally for her hand in marriage and presented her with a four-karat engagement ring. Soon married, the happy couple moved into a lovely beach home.

As part of Sally's dedication to health and fitness, she worked out every morning with Burt, her personal trainer and a dear trusted friend. Harry noticed that Burt was also exceptionally handsome and athletic, a man most women would find hard to resist. It was also clear that Sally and Burt shared a special relationship.

Rather than rejoicing that his wife had such a good friend, Harry expressed jealousy. At length, Harry asked Sally to get a new trainer. Taken aback by her husband's request, Sally was hurt and insulted. She was a loyal wife; Burt was a trusted pal.

Rather than embrace reassurance, Harry first threw a temper tantrum, then threw various objects. When the final piece of expensive crystal crashed against the wall, Sally wisely suggested professional marriage counseling.

Harry refused. Dismayed, Sally urged him to get individual counseling to deal with his self-created scenarios of expected betrayal. She was not, however, about to dismiss her dear friend due to Harry's delusions.

Formerly obsessed with having Sally, Harry was now obsessed with catching her in an extramarital affair. To accomplish this goal, he came to me.

"I am positive that Sally is having an affair with Burt," said Harry, and he hired my firm to watch her when he went on business trips, and whenever she was out of town shooting a picture.

"Sally is not having an affair with Burt," I reported back to him, "nor is she having an affair with anyone else." Harry didn't believe me. He was sure that Sally was outsmarting us.

His next plan: have us install hidden video cameras throughout the house. We decided that doing so would at least give him peace of mind, so we installed the cameras. Harry seemed pleased with his new toy and couldn't wait to review the tapes that he just knew would reveal Sally's deceitful behavior.

The tapes, of course, revealed only a happy, loyal, loving wife. Harry was blatantly disappointed. So convinced was he of her infidelity, he actually confronted her with non-existent evidence, insisting that he had proof of her affair with Burt.

That did it. She exploded in a rage of hurt and fury. "I've been a loyal and faithful wife," she said angrily. "How dare you say such a thing?"

"You're obviously more than just friends," countered Harry. "He's obviously handsome—"

"In case you haven't noticed," she snapped at him, "I am obviously a married woman, and Burt is obviously gay!"

Suddenly realizing the depths of his degrading and insulting behavior, Harry chased after her in tears. Over time, and with great effort and many apologies, he wooed her back for a second chance. He no longer had her followed nor did he obsess on imaginary indiscretions.

A few months later, Sally went to South America for a motion picture. An unexpected bout of dysentery afflicted the crew, and Sally avoided the runs by trotting home to Harry. On the flight back, Sally imagined what a fun surprise it would be when Harry saw her home so quickly.

Sally not only surprised Harry, she surprised Burt as well. The two men were having sex in her marital bed.

The stunned trio remained motionless for a moment. There was no way the men could avoid Sally's wilting gaze.

"Harry, you're having sex with Burt," she blurted out as if Harry were unaware of the act or the identity of his partner.

"Yes, I know who he is, honey," came Harry's calm reply.

Sally saw the look on Burt's face, and realized her friend mistakenly assumed that the homoerotic coupling happened with her foreknowledge and tacit approval.

"I've always been bisexual, honey," admitted Harry, as if any validation were required. "I guess I should have told you."

Sally filed for a divorce. Harry and Burt moved in together. I don't know if Burt remained Sally's trainer, but I'm sure their friendship was strained by the affair.

Harry's obsession with catching Sally having her non-existent affair with Burt is something only a psychologist could explain. From my experience as a private eye, sometimes when a person says, "I *know* my spouse is doing something wrong," what they really mean is "I don't really know anything." It is the fear of being right, plus the fear of being paranoid, that motivates them to take decisive action and find out the truth.

Some affairs are sloppy, ill-concealed violations of trust. Others are elaborate schemes, planned and executed with the precision of a professional heist.

The cleverest scheme ever devised by cheating husbands was created by a group of philandering businessmen in Los Angeles. As if with most acts of conspiratorial dishonesty, it eventually came crashing down, breaking hearts and destroying families in the process.

With much trepidation, the wife of a Los Angeles executive came to my office. It was all gut feelings on her part, she admitted, but she suspected her husband was having an affair. Interestingly, he displayed none of the primary telltale signs of cheating.

He often went out of town on business trips, and every time she called him up, he was always where he said he would be. If he said he was going to be on business in Texas, for example, he would leave her his itinerary with the phone numbers and addresses of all the hotels he would be staying on his trip. When she called, he would answer, and nothing seemed out of the ordinary. Despite outward appearances, the missus' intuition told her there was something amiss with the mister.

I took the case, and when he left for his next business trip, we followed him to the airport. He parked his car in a very conspicuous spot in the parking lot. If his wife looked for his car at the airport, she would find it easily.

No sooner did he lock his car, then an attractive young woman pulled up in a late-model vehicle. He got in the passenger side, and we tailed the pair all the way to a residence in Marina del Rey. We researched the property ownership and discovered it was in the names of the husband and the other woman.

From the husband's itinerary, we got the number of the hotel in Dallas, Texas, where he was supposedly staying. I called the number, and a woman answered, "Hilton Hotel, may I help you?"

"Yes, please connect me to the room of Dr. Lyle Jenson," I requested, making up the name on the spot.

"I'm sorry," she replied, "we have no one by that name registered."

"Please look again," I begged, "we have an emergency at the hospital. This is a matter of life or death, and this is the only number we have for Dr. Jensen."

The person put me on hold for a minute, and during those sixty seconds, I prayed that she wouldn't realize that my story was an obvious lie; there was no way that anyone would have given me that fake phone number. I was counting on the "life or death" ruse to push things in our favor.

When she came back on the line, she told the truth. "This is not actually the Hilton Hotel," she said nervously. "This is an answering service in Los Angeles where the calls are forwarded to. That's why we know Dr. Jensen is not here."

We traced the call from the call forwarding number back to Los Angeles, got the address of the answering service, and investigated the answering service's ownership. It did not take long for the entire scheme to unravel. The service was created specifically to create the illusion that these specific businessmen were out of town on work-related activities when they were actually having affairs in their own hometowns.

They would set up fictitious business trips. The phone numbers in those cities, all with proper area codes, were low-cost lines with automatic call forwarding back to the answering service in Los Angeles.

When the answering service received a call, the system told them where the call was coming from, to whose itinerary it related, and the procedure for contacting the person in event of an actual emergency, either by pager or at the love nest.

A little meeting was arranged between the cheating husband and a prospective client—me. I showed him the videotape of his mistress meeting him at the airport, displayed a copy of the property deed proving his co-ownership of his lover's home, and produced copies of checks he had personally signed to the WLFY Answering Service.

He didn't put up an argument or a fuss. He met his wife's divorce settlement conditions and she went on her way, as did he.

Before he left, I asked him one question. "What was the significance of WLFY?"

"Oh," he said with a smile, "WLFY stands for We Lie For You."

Chapter Two

How to Catch Loved Ones Cheating

Not all victims of cheating spouses hire a private detective. Some catch and confront the cheater on their own. You can confront your spouse or lover when you merely suspect they are cheating, or you can wait until you have overwhelming conclusive evidence.

Whether you want to confront someone with your suspicions or your facts, the approach is the same. Be clear in your own mind about the reason for the confrontation. Make sure you have a well-defined goal. If all you want to do is provoke a crisis with no plan for resolution or outcome, you are setting the stage for nothing but emotional disaster.

Whatever your desired outcome, you must avoid putting the other person in a situation where they feel forced to lie. What you want is the truth. The vast majorities of lying loved ones feel considerable guilt and shame for their behavior and will gladly be honest if they can do so without fear of humiliation or punishment.

The commonality that exists in all people is the need to tell the truth and relieve the unpleasant sense of guilt. Remember, most people lie for two basic reasons: fear of punishment and/or fear of embarrassment.

Eliminate the two reasons why people lie and, theoretically, they will tell you the truth. With the exception of sociopaths, psychopaths, and trained actors, people are dreadful liars. You can tell they are lying the moment they begin speaking.

There is one very basic reason liars are easily spotted: human beings are designed to only tell the truth. Telling a lie throws the entire human system into chaos, causing conflicts between the sympathetic and parasympathetic nervous systems. These two systems regulate the everyday functioning of the human body, including blood pressure, heart rate, skin response, eye movements, and everything else.

The disruptions caused by the lie can be measured as if it were an earthquake. The lie's negative effect impacts speech, gestures, and coordination. When someone tells a lie, they change. They have no control over this transformation, as it is a deep-seated automatic response. In short, the liar's behavior suddenly changes.

Some of the most common symptoms exhibited by someone in the midst of a lie are almost clichés: they can't look you in the eyes; they begin sweating, blushing, fidgeting, and/or smirking.

The way professionals detect liars is to look for changes in behavior. Both body language and speech patterns change when a person lies. If you are going to play detective, pay close attention to these primary clues.

If you're dealing with a bad liar who was caught off guard, they often attempt to buy time by repeating the question before every answer. For example, if you ask a liar what they did last night and they don't want to tell you the truth, they may answer in a manner such as this: "What did I do last night? I went to a movie. Who did I go with? I went with Cousin Rob."

Liars are not trained professional actors, nor are they innovative masters of improvisation worthy of one-woman or one-man shows on Broadway. They tend to stutter and hesitate. After all, they are amateurs suddenly expected to improvise as if they were professionals.

Liars will also provide far more information and explanation than any truthful person would offer. So, when a wife goes off on a tangent about how she never got your message but she did get a weird message on her voicemail that made her laugh, you might have to ask her to revert to the topic at hand.

Politicians, not surprisingly, use this technique quite often. Sadly, many interviewers allow them to get away with it. One broadcast journalist famed for never allowing liars to avoid the issue was Ted Koppel of ABC. If a person avoided his "yes or no" question by giving a lengthy off-topic answer, Koppel would respond, "That's very interesting, but you did not answer the question. I repeat, did you or did you not…"

Look for inconsistencies. If parts of the story don't add up, keep asking for clarification. Don't badger the person; simply ask for explanations. It is always easier to tell the truth because there is less to remember—lies are too complex to remember in complete detail.

Some liars will overcompensate by saying, "If you don't believe me, give me a lie detector test." If they don't offer, you can suggest it. Normally in the heat of the confrontation, they will agree to take the test, never thinking that you would go through with it. If you decide to go through with it, be aware that while polygraphs have a reported eighty-seven percent accuracy rate, results can be manipulated. There are even instructions online on how to beat a polygraph test.

A woman contacted me one afternoon and said she suspected her husband of cheating on her. She called him at work the previous night, and an employee said that her husband left work early, around 4:30 p.m. When her husband returned home at 10:30 that night, she asked him where he had been. He replied, "I was at work."

"I called your work," she informed him, "and they told me that you left at 4:30."

"Nonsense," replied her husband forcefully. "If you don't believe me, I'll take a lie detector test."

She called me the next morning and set up an appointment for six that night. When they arrived at my office, he was a nervous wreck.

After some informal discussion, he told me that he owned a trucking company and he would like to hire me to conduct polygraph tests on his employees. I told him we would discuss that after the test.

"You don't understand," he told me. "I'm willing to pay you fifty thousand dollars."

He and I both knew that the union to which his employees belonged prohibited polygraph testing. In truth, he wasn't allowed to have his employees tested at all. What he was really doing was offering to pay me fifty thousand to not conduct any testing.

"That fifty grand covers tonight too," he said, giving me a sly wink.

A tempting bribe is a bribe nonetheless. He was offering me money to lie and say he was telling the truth. I asked him why he was offering me so much money.

"Hell," he replied, "it's cheaper than a divorce."

"I think we can dispense with the polygraph test," I said with a smile.

When we rejoined his wife, my happy briber had a rude surprise. Instead of clearing his name, I revealed his generous offer.

"That's a lie," he lied.

"I tape-recorded our conversation," I responded calmly. "I'm sure you'll recognize your own voice."

"The hell with it," he barked and stormed out of my office. His wife thanked me and asked for a referral to a good divorce attorney.

In summary, remember these essential clues regarding lying behavior:

- A person who is lying to you will avoid making eye contact.
- Hands touching their face, throat, and mouth. Touching or scratching the nose or behind their ear. Not likely to touch their chest and/or heart with an open hand.
- Timing and duration of emotional gestures and emotions are off a normal pace. The display of emotion is delayed, stays longer than it would naturally, then stops suddenly.
- Timing is off between emotions, gestures and expressions, and words. Example: someone says, "I love it!" when receiving a gift, and then smiles after making that statement rather than at the same time the statement is made.
- Gestures and expressions don't match the verbal statement, such as frowning when saying, "I love you."
- Expressions are limited to mouth movements when someone is faking emotions (like happy, surprised, sad, awe) instead of the whole face. Example: when someone smiles naturally, their whole face is involved (jaw/cheek movement, eyes and forehead push down, etc.).
- A guilty person gets defensive. An innocent person will often go on the offensive.
- A liar is uncomfortable facing his questioner/accuser and may turn his head or body away.
- A liar might unconsciously place objects (book, coffee cup, etc.) between themselves and you.
- A liar will use your words to answer a question. When asked, "Did you eat the last cookie?", the liar answers, "No, I did not eat the last cookie."
- A statement with a contraction is more likely to be truthful: "I didn't do it" instead of "I did not have sex with that woman." Liars sometimes avoid lying by

not making direct statements. They imply answers instead of denying something directly.

- The guilty person may speak more than required, adding unnecessary details to convince you; they are not comfortable with silence or pauses in the conversation.
- A liar may leave out pronouns and speak in a monotonous tone. When a truthful statement is made, the pronoun is emphasized as much or more than the rest of the words in a statement.
- Words may be garbled and spoken softly, and syntax and grammar may be off. In other words, his sentences will likely be muddled rather than emphasized.

If you believe someone is lying, change the subject of the conversation quickly. A liar follows along willingly and becomes more relaxed. The guilty wants the subject changed; an innocent person may be confused by the sudden change in topics and will want to go back to the previous subject.

The best way to deal with liars is to not deal with them in the first place. You *can* avoid deceitful relationships. You can prevent getting involved with someone who will cheat and lie to you if you do the necessary investigative work beforehand.

Most of us would not buy a business before checking out the company. We would carefully examine the assets, accounts receivable, accounts payable, and a list of clients or contacts. We would be very careful before entering into any type of financial situation.

When a new person enters our life, we should be equally careful. Before you hand them your heart, home, and bank account, make sure they are being honest.

Thanks to modern technology and the internet, full background checks are easily available and affordable. For example, peoplesearch.com offers "romantic investigations" from sixty to ninety dollars. Security companies will also conduct background checks on potential employees. Whether romantic or business, background checks are essentially the same when it comes to information. The report you receive should contain the following:

- credit report
- criminal record
- social security number
- municipal and civil litigation as plaintiff or defendant
- small-claims court actions
- evictions
- bankruptcy listings
- notes of default on loans
- foreclosures
- tax liens

I would also ask if the company conducts behavioral analysis interviews with prospective employees or potential husbands/wives. It may sound presumptuous to request this from your intended spouse, but it could be a lifesaver.

The cost should run no more than seventy-five to one hundred dollars, and if the company is professional, they can give you information about the person that isn't found in public records—information provided directly by the person being interviewed. You can learn of theft from previous employers, drug problems, drinking problems, undetected crimes, reasons for leaving previous jobs, military history, and more. All of this information comes from the applicant themselves. We call this the hope-and-fear syndrome. They hope if they tell the investigator the truth, they will recommend the applicant for the job. They are afraid if they attempt to lie, they will be detected and turned down.

If you choose to conduct the background check yourself, you may find things overlooked by peoplesearch.com, other online firms, or even some security companies. This isn't to say that their searches are not professional; it simply means that the personal approach often uncovers more.

The fallout of not doing a background check can be devastating. I can think of no more horrific example than the following true story, revealed here for the first time anywhere. Brace yourself, this is one wild ride!

THE CENTER

by Fred Wolfson as told to Burl Barer

The Center for Constitutional Law and Justice was based in North Hollywood, California. The non-profit organization opened its doors in 1991 and business was booming.

The Center was the mastermind of entrepreneur Fred Sebastian. It was a civil rights organization that represented clients who couldn't afford an attorney. Clients would pay whatever they could up front (usually two or three thousand dollars) and The Center would handle the case from there.

In seven short months, The Center represented over sixteen hundred defendants. The Center for Constitutional Law and Justice consisted of six attorneys, including Mr. Sebastian, and two paralegals.

The newest of the attorneys was a recent hire named Dennis Palmieri. When he saw the ad in the National Law Journal, he knew it was too good to pass up.

The ad read, "Established civil rights law firm is in the process of opening offices in every state before December of this year. If you have a liberal outlook and a desire to try controversial civil and criminal cases with national impact and enjoy recognition and publicity, call The Center For Constitutional Law And Justice and ask for Fred Sebastian."

Dennis jumped at the chance.

He was about as liberal as one could get, and the spotlight was something he never shied away from. He was hired after only one interview and immediately went to work.

Dennis liked his new boss. Fred Sebastian was his kind of lawyer. He was an attorney who wrote his own rules and Dennis, who was a bit of an eccentric himself, could relate.

When Fred gave him his first assignment, Dennis was eager to impress but it would not be easy. The Los Angeles Riots had just taken place and Fred Sebastian had been watching with a keen eye.

The four men who'd attacked Reginald Denny were chosen to stand trial for the hundreds who'd burned and pillaged the City of Los Angeles. This was exactly the high-profile kind of case that could put the organization on the front pages of every newspaper in the country, which is what Fred Sebastian had coveted from day one.

Dennis Palmieri's assignment, find Damian Williams' family and persuade them to let The Center take on the case pro bono. Damian was the star of the LA Four.

It was he who'd hit Denny in the face with a brick and Sebastian could taste the publicity already. Dennis knew it would not be easy but the determined attorney vowed to give it his all.

Dennis had no idea where the family lived other than it was somewhere in South Central LA. With no other choice, he began the search and literally went door to door in the neighborhood asking if this was the Williams' household.

After two days of searching, he found what he was looking for. Georgiana Williams had been beside herself. The single mother of four wanted desperately to help her youngest child, Damian.

If he had truly done what the news media was portraying, then he would pay, but she at least wanted the assurance that her son would receive a fair trial. A public defender was out of the question. A high-powered attorney was beyond her means. She tried but the NAACP also offered no help.

She was alone and confused and not sure what to do next. A knock at the door solved the problem. The timing could not have been better. Dennis Palmieri and The Center for Constitutional Law and Justice must have been sent from heaven. There was no other logical explanation.

She immediately signed on the dotted line and gave them the case. She had done her job. Her son was now in the best possible legal hands and better yet, it was free. A cross between the ACLU and Amnesty International was the way Mr. Palmieri had described his law firm. It was perfect. Georgiana Williams could now rest easy. Her son would get a fair trial.

Private investigator Fred Wolfson was sitting in his office when the call came in. He had just finished months of tedious work on the Rodney King Case, working for the Los Angeles Police Department Protective League as a civilian investigator. He was looking forward to taking some much-needed time off. It was not to be.

An attorney named Dennis Palmieri was on the line and he was asking for the investigator's help in the defense of Damian Williams. Fred was wary about accepting the job. During the King investigation, his family had received numerous death threats. He thought it was finally over and put to rest. Now this.

Fred agreed to work on the case under two conditions. First, he got to interview Damian Williams personally. Second, if Damian was lying, he wanted no part of it. Palmieri agreed and after Fred's initial interview with Damian at the Los Angeles County Jail, he was brought on board as the chief investigator for the defense.

The private investigator's first meeting with Fred Sebastian did not go well. From minute one, the investigator knew something wasn't right. The founder of The Center was nervous, evasive, and seemed to have everything on his mind other than the defense of Damian Williams.

Fred Wolfson is an expert in human behavior with degrees to back it up and he knew immediately this was a man with something to hide. Deciding to pry, the investigator asked Sebastian about his background. The answer he received would send up a major red flag.

Sebastian told the investigator that he used to work clandestine operations for the CIA. Wrong! Coincidentally, Fred Wolfson himself was an ex-employee of the federal government and he knew from experience that no ex or current agent of the CIA would ever come out and simply admit it.

The nation was watching as the preliminary hearing of Damian Williams began. The Center for Constitutional Law and Justice was now firmly on the map and was the absolute talk of the town. Fred Sebastian had gained so much notoriety, he was now hosting his own radio call-in talk show called *Civil Liberties*, which solicited even more business and donations for The Center. Life was good and Mr. Sebastian's business was flourishing. Everything would have been perfect except for one small fly in the ointment— Fred Wolfson.

Sebastian's CIA comment had bothered him immensely and he decided before going any further, to check out The Center and its mastermind. If the investigator was going to work with them, he didn't want any surprises coming back to haunt him later.

The lack of progress Palmieri and Sebastian were making at the preliminary hearing was also leaving a bad taste in his mouth. The strategy they were using in the defense of Damian Williams was bizarre, to say the least. On the morning of the initial arrest, Damian had made a taped confession of his involvement in the beating of Reginald Denny. It was quite damaging to his case. But the defense had an out.

According to a procedural rule, the defense has the right to ask the court to suppress a piece of prejudicial information. But it can make this request only once in the course of a case.

Dennis Palmieri believed that if Damian's statement was played in open court, he would be deemed guilty by anyone who heard it; most importantly, potential jurors. He immediately filed a motion to suppress the tape but there was a bitter argument. Fred Sebastian disagreed with the attorney and ordered Palmieri to withdraw the motion.

Dennis knew it was a mistake but was threatened with his job and finally gave in and withdrew the motion. Supporters of the LA Four were livid. The Black community was up in arms and telling anyone who would listen that Damian Williams' attorney was obviously prejudiced and for some reason doing everything in his power to screw up the case.

Wolfson had seen enough. He intensified his investigation of The Center and of Mr. Fred Sebastian. He didn't like what he found. The investigator's instincts had been on the money.

According to the secretary of state and the City of Los Angeles, The Center for Constitutional Law and Justice didn't even exist. There was no business license. They were not registered as a non-profit organization. It wasn't even a corporation. Fred immediately called Dennis Palmieri and withdrew from the case. He told him something wasn't right and refused to be a part of it.

Dennis accepted his resignation but didn't really give it much thought. He was much too immersed in the hearing and figured hiring another investigator was just another item added to his already long list of things to do.

It finally appeared the private investigator would be able to take his long-awaited time off. He was burnt out and couldn't remember the last time he was actually able to relax. A phone call changed his plans. It was Fred Sebastian on the line. This man just would not go away. Sebastian said he was sorry that Fred had withdrawn from the Williams case but wanted to make him another offer.

He asked Fred if he'd be interested in working a seizure case for The Center. He said that a twelve-million-dollar jet had been seized from one of his clients by the federal government. If The Center could retrieve the plane, its comission would be in the neighborhood of four million dollars. Sebastian offered to split the commission with Fred if he could simply find the location of the plane.

Fred's first question was why the government had seized the jet in the first place. Sebastian unbelievably told him it was none of his business! With no intention of working for The Center or Sebastian, Fred played along anyway, knowing it was now time to find out once and for all exactly who Mr. Fred Sebastian really was.

The first thing he did was run the name of the man Sebastian had given him as the owner of the airplane. Fred was not the least bit surprised to find out that the owner was a major figure in the world of organized crime.

The preliminary hearing of Damian Williams was finally winding down. Dennis Palmieri had been writing his closing summation for weeks and he was at last ready. Unfortunately, he may have been too ready.

Once he began his closing argument, he refused to end it. He went on and on and on. They took the morning break. Then he continued. They broke for lunch. Then he continued again. Soon it was time for the afternoon break. There was no end in sight. The courtroom was stunned. Palmieri was babbling and not making a whole lot of sense.

Maybe it had finally caught up with him...or maybe he had been crazy from the beginning. Fred Sebastian couldn't believe what he was hearing. The airwaves were filled with stories of the crazed defense attorney and his summation from hell. Sebastian was beside himself and frantically grabbed a file folder stuffed with old resumes. Surprisingly, he had never actually taken the time to read Dennis Palmieri's.

Sebastian had been so excited to hire the lawyer when he agreed to go door to door and bring in the Damian Williams Case, he hadn't even bothered glancing at it. For the first time, he decided to read it now and was shocked at what he saw.

Palmieri, according to Sebastian, stated on his resume that he'd worked on expeditions to Mars and had also helped establish mining colonies on the moon. The rest of the resume was equally bizarre, and Sebastian knew he'd made a serious error in judgment. The only answer was to get to the courthouse and rectify it before it was too late.

Sebastian, in what is believed to be a first, burst into the courtroom that day and tried to fire his attorney mid-summation. He informed the judge that Dennis Palmieri was off the case and would no longer be affiliated with The Center for Constitutional Law and Justice. But for the seriousness of the moment, it would have been a comic scene: a windy lawyer getting the axe in the middle of his closing argument!

The judge thought he had seen it all but this one took the cake. He finally decided to ignore both Sebastian and Palmieri and left the decision up to Damian. Damian's decision was to let Palmieri finish his summation.

Fred Wolfson shifted his investigation of Sebastian into high gear. His findings not only exceeded his own expectations, but they were also mind-boggling. Fred Sebastian was not even a lawyer. The founder of The Center for Constitutional Law and Justice had no legal background. The American Bar Association had never heard of him.

Practicing law without a license was the least of his problems. Fred Sebastian wasn't even Fred Sebastian! His real name was Fred Celani. It got better.

Celani did in fact have extensive experience with the law—but not as a lawyer. Celani had spent many occasions over the years in prison for operating various cons all over the country.

In New York, there was a bogus riverfront development deal. In Illinois, he posed as a tax lawyer and mechanical engineer. He was charged with fraud and racketeering and released on a ten thousand dollar bond. While awaiting trial he opened a bogus real estate consulting firm and cheated investors out of a hundred thousand dollars in just four months.

When Celani was released from prison in 1991, he immediately rented office space and opened The Center for Constitutional Law and Justice.

This would prove to be not only his biggest con to date but quite possibly the biggest con in the history of our country. Mr. Celani scammed an entire nation and we fell for it, hook, line, and sinker.

If not for Fred Wolfson, he may very well have gotten away with it. Fred called the Justice Department and gave them what he had on Sebastian. It was hard for them to believe that the lawyer in charge of possibly the biggest case in Los Angeles' history was a complete fraud, but there it was in black and white, and it was undeniable. Nobody could understand how Sebastian had pulled it off for so long, but they all agreed on one point: it was time to get Celani off the streets once and for all.

The FBI set up its own con. One of The Center's other clients was a suspected drug trafficker in Little Rock, Arkansas. Upon questioning the suspect's wife, the FBI learned that Mr. Sebastian had let it be known that it might be possible for The Center to get the woman's husband off if she gave Sebastian fifty thousand dollars to bribe a federal official. The timing couldn't be better. The feds wired the women and on two occasions, she got Sebastian to repeat the offer, only now it was on tape.

When Sebastian flew to Little Rock and accepted the money, the feds moved in quickly and it was finally over. The Center for Constitutional Law and Justice was officially closed with the California State Bar taking over its still open cases, which numbered close to a thousand.

While The Center was open for business, estimates are they took in approximately four million dollars, though no one knows the exact number.

When Celani was residing in an Arkansas prison cell awaiting trial, he said that it was time to come clean and supplied authorities with the following information. Celani claimed he was a secret agent acting only on government orders to get the Damian Williams case and do whatever he could to sabotage it.

"The Bush Administration," he said, "wanted to prove there was lawlessness in L.A., and it was out of control. If they could create this racial struggle, they knew that the law and order vote would come to their side."

Damian Williams quickly hired a new attorney who immediately asked that all charges be dropped because of what had transpired with The Center. Congresswoman Maxine Waters agreed and said, "The case has been so tainted, it's beyond being tampered with."

The implications in the legal community regarding The Center are overwhelming. The Center handled over sixteen hundred criminal cases. In not one of those cases was a plea bargain accepted, a reduced sentence achieved, or a not guilty verdict awarded.

Fred Sebastian pulled off the con of all time. He not only scammed Los Angeles but an entire nation as well. There are dozens of loose ends still dangling in the Sebastian/Celani story. It will take many years to clean up the mess. Was there a conspiracy? Was the government involved? Doubtful, yet some pieces of the puzzle do have trouble fitting.

Celani claims when he was released from Terminal Island Prison in 1991, he was recruited by Ron Brown, then chairman of the Democratic National Committee. Supposedly the Democrats were so desperate to win California in the upcoming presidential election, they hired him to help sabotage prominent Republican Conservatives. Using The Center as a front, Celani said he followed Representative Bob Dornan and bugged the offices of talk-show host Rush Limbaugh and others.

He says he was then instructed by federal agents to solicit the Damian Williams case so that they could insure the reading of Damian's confession in open court.

"My orders were to completely fuck-up the case," says Celani. "I was told to countermand Palmieri and bury our client, which I did. With that accomplished, I was sent to Little Rock to thwart the murder of a federal judge. The money I took was all part of the cover-up but an overzealous FBI agent who was out of the loop had me arrested. When I called my contact in Washington, I was told to sit tight and it would all be taken care of. Now he won't accept my calls, which is why I have chosen to come out and tell the truth."

Celani's tale seems a desperate alibi, but there are indications that it isn't one hundred percent fiction.

UNITED STATES V. CELANI

While on parole following incarceration for prior fraud and racketeering charges, Frederick George Celani told a convicted felon, Leland Glasco, that he could get Glasco released from prison by bribing public officials. Glasco and his wife cooperated with the FBI, and Celani eventually was charged with seven counts of wire fraud and one count of inducing a person to travel in interstate commerce in execution of a scheme to defraud. Celani was convicted following a jury trial, and he appealed his conviction.

Prior to trial, Celani claimed that he began working as an undercover FBI agent in 1986 and 1987. While in prison on the fraud charge he was still serving in 1992, he learned that Leland Glasco had threatened the life of a federal judge, and he pursued his bribery scheme with the Glascos at the direction of the government to divert Glasco from carrying out his threat. The government moved to preclude that defense.

The district court permitted Celani to assert the public authority defense at trial. The parties stipulated that Celani had provided information about a fellow inmate to Peter Wacks, an FBI agent, in 1987, and Celani testified in his own behalf, asserting that Agent Wacks had directed him to pursue the bribery scheme, including the acts charged in the indictment.

While permitting Celani to pursue this defense, the district court denied him access to his entire Bureau of Prisons file, quashed his subpoenas for the testimony of certain prison officers and to produce confidential FBI files, and excluded evidence of the details of his work for Agent Wacks and his contacts with a House of Representatives committee in 1986.

After reviewing the relevant government files prior to trial, the court concluded that the details of Celani's pre-1992 dealings with the government on matters unrelated to the Glascos were unnecessary to his defense and had the potential to confuse the jury.

On appeal, Celani argued that the district court's review of the confidential government files precluded him from establishing the materiality of the sealed evidence, and that the evidentiary rulings violated his Sixth Amendment rights by prejudicially depriving him of evidence that would have bolstered his defense.

To prove Sixth Amendment right-to-compulsory-process violation, the defendant must show that the evidence was material and favorable to the defense.

Celani was unable to do so.

In the beginning, federal officials denied any knowledge of Fred Celani. Today their story has changed. A document has been uncovered that adds a shred of credibility to Celani's case. It's a letter addressed to Celani from the

House Subcommittee on Oversight and Investigations, dated September 30, 1986 and is personally signed by Representative John Dingell, D-Michigan.

The letter promises the Committee will never use any classified information obtained and supplied by Celani directly or indirectly to his detriment.

This is the first piece of evidence linking Celani with the federal government, but subcommittee member Dennis Fitzgibbons admits that Celani was contacted in 1986 in connection with an ongoing investigation of government contracting but says the information Celani provided was false, so the matter was dropped, as was Celani.

Celani's conviction was affirmed by the appeals court, and America's supreme con man was once again behind bars.

CHAPTER THREE

THE DATE CHECKLIST

You have a date with someone. What do you know about this person? Assign a score of five points for each item that you know.

1. Do you know their real name?
2. Home address?
3. Place of work?
4. Where their family lives?
5. Have you met their family?
6. Medical background?
7. Yearly income?
8. Credit history?
9. Favorite food?
10. Personal habits?
11. Sexual habits?
12. Litigation history?
13. Drinking habits?
14. Drug habits?
15. Arrest record?
16. Old flames?
17. Old flames with something bad to say?
18. Date of birth?
19. Military history?
20. Level of education?

100 to 85 points: you know the person well. Good for you.

80 to 70 points: you know the person well enough for a second date.

65 to 50 points: have another conversation with them on the phone.

45 to 30 points: ask more questions, and get more answers.

25 points or below: you must have picked this person's name out of a phonebook

Sad but true, even when people know they are linked to a loser, they refuse to break the chain of self-destruction.

A famous Hollywood producer hired me to check out his daughter's intended spouse. The two became engaged only one week prior. The producer, however, knew a bad actor when he saw one. "This guy is a charmer," he told me. "And I've had bad feelings about him from the start. He's a sharp-dressing, good-looking, tall blond fellow with big blue eyes. He drives a new Jaguar convertible and lives in a swanky apartment in Marina del Rey, a part of Los Angeles located near the ocean."

The guy, Bill, presented the daughter with a three-and-a-half karat diamond ring and asked for her hand in marriage. The father tried to talk his daughter, Betty, out of the marriage, but to no avail.

We started our investigation by running Bill's license plate and discovered he didn't own it or even lease the car. It was a rental. The information on the car rental application was extremely interesting. The employer Bill referenced on the rental agreement was bogus. The background investigation revealed the following items:

He was expelled from school in the tenth grade. His first arrest as an adult occurred on Bill's twenty-first birthday when he was arrested for drunk and disorderly conduct.

Bill's first marriage occurred soon thereafter, at the age of twenty-two. That marriage lasted fourteen months. After Bill had fathered a child, he deserted his wife. He was arrested once again for spousal abuse after marrying his second wife at twenty-five and served ten days of community service. He returned to his wife and was once again arrested for battery after starting a fight with his neighbor and attacking him with a rake.

His original charge was assault with a deadly weapon. After plea bargaining, he pled guilty to a misdemeanor battery and served twenty-one days in county jail and was ordered to pay restitution to the neighbor in the amount of fifteen thousand dollars for damages. The neighbor sued Bill and received a judgement in the amount of ninety-five thousand dollars. His neighbor never saw a penny of the money.

Bill deserted his second wife and left town, starting a new life in the armed services. His new career lasted sixteen months when he received a dishonorable discharge for possession of a controlled substance. Bill was attracted to the wealth of Beverly Hills, and selected that zip code as his new target. He wanted a wealthy woman, and Beverly Hills was where he'd find her.

He needed money for more than amusement—he had a state tax lien and one hundred twenty-six thousand dollars in outstanding debt. Creditors were looking for him under three social security numbers.

Bill's litigation record looked much like his criminal conviction record. He was in and out of court as a plaintiff and defendant; he sued people and was sued a total of thirty-two times—everything from small-claims actions to a past judgement from which he fled. He also filed numerous workman's compensation claims against his previous employers. He owed his two ex-wives back child support, which he had not made a payment on. Overall, in the game of life, he was a loser.

Our client was astonished at the information we had uncovered and paid us the same day we dropped off the report. He couldn't wait to show his daughter and save her from making a terrible mistake. Betty did not respond to the information in the same way as her father.

Just to prove how wrong her father was, she said that she and Bill were going to elope to Las Vegas the next day. To punish him for his act of interfering in her life, she said that he would never see her again and never see his grandchildren. She ran off to Las Vegas and two horrid years of abuse.

She had a thirteen-month-old baby and was pregnant with her second child when she called her family to plead for forgiveness. She told a tale of how Bill would come home in a drunken stupor and could never find a job that met his qualifications. No employer would put up with him and neither would she.

She claimed that she would have come home sooner but that it was difficult to save face in her family's eyes. Her family raised the two children as she tried to get her life back together. Soon after, she met Alan, a man who was not as good looking as Bill, but he also didn't have any of Bill's problems. They were married in a small church service after we had given him a clean bill of health. This time, the daughter was thankful for her father's generosity.

The moral of the story is simple: it doesn't matter how much information you have going into a relationship, it's what you do with the information that counts. Most of the information you need is a matter of public record and is as easy to look up as going to the public library.

1. *ARE THEY MARRIED?*

Easy. Most states keep marriage records for years and it is a matter of public record. For example, in California, all you need is the bride's or groom's name and approximately how old they are and you can pull up all previous marriages. It is good to know if the number is excessive so you know what you're getting into.

2. ARE THEY REALLY DIVORCED?

No problem. Guess what? Divorce records are also a matter of public record. In most states, divorces are heard in superior court and are filed by the respondent's or petitioner's name. All you have to do is call the superior court in the county where you live and ask how to access their records. Normally, a clerk will talk you through the process. It may take as long as a couple of hours and they may require a copy fee per page. Tell them you are not interested in the entire proceeding. All you need is the date of the trial, the respondent, and the final decree.

If you research the records and do not find your beloved's claimed divorcee, they still might be telling the truth. In some states, only the final divorce decree is on file, and may take as long as six months to show up. If you have any questions about the state you live in, ask to speak to the county clerk's office and they may be able to help you.

3. WHERE DO THEY LIVE?

Once again, this is in the public record. If they own property or vacant land, the county recorder will have a record of the property, along with a storehouse of information. You will discover things like sales price, date of sale, number of bedrooms and baths, and if it has a pool. It will tell what type of heating and air conditioning it has, how much taxes are, and, most of the time, it will give you a home phone number. Some states offer more information than others, but, all in all, you will find information that the public is not aware is available to them.

Other things that are important are also a matter of public record and are easily accessible.

MUNICIPAL AND SUPERIOR COURT LITIGATION, both as a plaintiff and defendant.

If the person is prone to litigation or is being sued by everyone, watch out. It shows a history of problems that you want to stay away from. It also shows you how they run their lives, if they're responsible, or if they take every chance they can to not pay their bills or stand behind contracts they have signed. Most people have appeared in court at some time in their lives, but someone who knows the court snack bar person by their first name might drag you through the legal system, giving you an experience you will never forget.

SMALL CLAIMS ACTIONS

Some people love to sue others and utilize the small-claims courts to settle petty disputes. In some states, you can sue someone up to twenty-five hundred dollars. In other states, the same thinking applies to small-claims courts that apply to municipal and superior courts.

UNLAWFUL DETAINERS

This is a term used to kick someone off a property; for example, someone who doesn't pay their rent. It once again establishes a lifestyle you might consider staying away from.

BANKRUPTCY LISTINGS

All you need is the person's name and social security number for any bankruptcy listing. Just go down to the local federal courthouse and ask the clerk where you can find bankruptcy listings. In some courthouses, if the clerk isn't too busy, they will pull the records for you. This information is available for a seven-year period.

NOTICES OF DEFAULT

Notices of default indicate when someone has lost a property or any collateralized loan because of non-payment to a lender.

FORECLOSURES occur when you actually lose your property to a lender.

FEDERAL, STATE, AND COUNTY TAX LIENS

If you don't pay taxes to the government, they put a lien against you for taxes due, plus interest and penalties. So, if someone looked pretty good on the surface and you find out they have liens against them, that excess baggage may hinder your relationship by making you pay off their debts to the government.

JUDGEMENTS

These are similar to liens. The only difference is that the money is owed to an individual or company rather than the government.

A Social Security Number Check

This will reveal all the people using a specific social security number and will include past and current addresses of the subject and may include any applicable spouse's name. As an example, 1233-38-1111: Robert/Mary Doe, 123 Any Street, Anywhere USA 00090. Cost: approximately twenty-five dollars.

Now you know how to find out the truth about your dates. But remember, nobody is perfect. Don't get carried away.

I was hired by a woman in publishing who had been a career woman all of her life. At middle age, she shifted values. Things that were important to her ten years before just didn't seem as important today.

While she was striving to get to the top of her profession, working six and seven days a week, she had put her personal life on hold and didn't have time for dating. But once she achieved her goals, she felt that life had passed her by, and then decided to look for a husband and start a family.

This career woman embarked into the single world, résumé in hand, as she looked at marriage as a business deal and she wanted the upper hand.

She contacted our office to check out potential dates, to avoid wasting time with men who had a checkered past. She gave us her qualifications for a man she would accept as a date or a potential spouse.

She gave me specific instructions, outlining exactly what she was looking for. "Anyone not meeting these qualifications," she insisted, "is not acceptable." She would screen them on the first date and then send me the information to make sure that he met her qualifications. Here is what she specified:

1. A man between the ages of thirty-eight and forty-five.
2. He must be a college graduate.

3. He must not have children, either from an ex-wife or out of wedlock.
4. His yearly income must be at least $112,000.
5. He must be a doctor, lawyer, or at least vice president of a major corporation.
6. He must not have any history of substance abuse, alcohol, drugs, or smoking.
7. He must have a clean arrest record.
8. He must be willing to sign a prenuptial agreement.
9. He must be genetically pure with no history of mental disorders or genetic illness.
10. He must keep himself in a professional manner by the way he dresses and not live in disarray.
11. His family bloodline must have no history of cancer or heart disease.
12. He must own his own home.
13. He must not have more than one failed marriage.
14. He must be well read.
15. He must be worldly and have traveled extensively.
16. He must possess good manners.
17. He must be between 5'11" and 6'1".
18. His weight must be in proportion to his height.
19. He must enjoy the arts.
20. His friends must be cultured.
21. He must enjoy traveling, but mustn't camp or go hiking.
22. He must drive a late-model foreign car, such as a Mercedes or BMW.
23. He must enjoy French, Italian, and Greek cooking.

The list did not end there. She had over sixty items mandated. Despite my best efforts on her behalf, she met and fell in love with an out-of-work house painter whose primary characteristic was that he was a heck of a nice guy. They have two children and are living happily in her home.

He is an ex-football player and still plays on the weekends with his friends. He is a great father and husband.

Some spouses, of course, are not nice. Following a divorce, they can be irrational and vindictive. Sometimes, they kidnap their own children.

CHAPTER FOUR

KIDNAPPED CHILDREN

We were hired by a father who had obtained custody of his children, ages six and nine, through a long custody battle. His children attended a private school in a wealthy part of Los Angeles. When a child is enrolled in this school, the parents must give the school a list of people who are authorized to pick the children up after or during school. Even though he had won custody of the children, he had forgotten to remove his wife's name from the list.

One day in November, she decided to abduct the children. The ex-wife went to the school at about 9:15 a.m. and told the principal that the children's grandmother had passed away and that she was going to take the children back east for the funeral. Then the principal checked the list and saw that ex-wife was authorized to remove the children from school. The principal asked for a picture ID to verify that she was, in fact, the children's mother. The school then released the children to their mother.

The mother had developed an elaborate scheme to hide the children. She had told her mother what she was about to do but didn't tell her where she was taking the children. If her mother needed to get in touch with her, she could beep her on a worldwide pager, punch in the number of the payphone that she was calling from, and she would call her back.

She left the same day for South America via Mexico, along with her two children. She made five stops before reaching her final destination. Her family was wealthy and had supplied her with money so she didn't have to use credit cards. She paid for everything in cash.

When we were called on the case, she had a three-week head start on us. Even though we checked the normal channels, there was no sign of the lady and her children. Our only hope was the grandmother, who lived in L.A. She would not talk to us and threatened to get a restraining order if we persisted in our efforts.

We believed the grandmother knew the location of her daughter and grandchildren, but would not lead to their whereabouts. We tried surveillance to no avail.

We had to be a little smarter than her if we were going to find these children.

While we were researching the ages of the children, we discovered that the nine-year-old had a birthday coming up in the end of December. So we had to act fast. We flew back to New York and met with an electronics expert who was an outcast from the CIA.

This man had electronic devices that were beyond James Bond's wildest dreams. He made each device himself in his workshop. We explained our problem and asked if there was a tracking device that could locate the children. He assured us that there was and that the cost would be six thousand dollars and would take three weeks to develop.

We asked if the device could be made in a week for eight thousand dollars. He said there would be no problem; I suspect it was something he had already made and on the shelf.

It arrived in two days, together with directions on how to use it. It was an electronic piano implanted with a tracking device that was powered by the batteries of the piano. It was a working model that actually played music.

We called our contact and asked if he knew where the device was now. He came within half a mile of our location. We also asked what would happen if the device got held up in customs somewhere. He explained that the piano also had a charging unit with it. It could be plugged into a 120- or 220-volt outlet, depending on the location. The batteries that were installed were rechargeable and would be like new within eight hours. We were satisfied.

We went to great efforts to wrap this instrument first in birthday paper, then in heavy brown shipping paper. We sent the piano to the grandmother and requested that she ship it to the nine-year-old for her birthday. We signed an uncle's name, the brother of the father, who was in on what we were doing. We also left off any return address, so that the piano could not be shipped back.

One week later, we received a call from New York, advising us that the package was moving. We were hoping it was headed in the right direction and was not being sent to a Goodwill facility. Our eight-thousand-dollar toy was on an airplane headed for its destination.

It moved slowly at times. We wondered how quickly it would reach its final destination. It landed in Brazil at the Rio airport. It then sat in customs for three days. The signal was getting weaker as the batteries were running down. It finally stopped transmitting and we lost contact with our expensive toy.

We were discouraged, but our contact once again assured us that once the unit was plugged in, we would know the exact location of the children.

Three days later, we started to receive a weak signal, but as the day went on, the signal grew in strength. The piano had landed in Porto Alegre, a small town south of Rio de Janeiro on the coast of the Atlantic Ocean.

We checked with our legal counsel to determine if our court order would be honored in Brazil. We were told that American court orders had no value in custody battles that occurred in civil court. So we had to plan our strategy to get the children home safely.

We chartered a private jet to take us to Brazil and landed in Rio. There were three of us—the father, my large investigator, and myself. Once in Brazil, we checked with the local authorities to ascertain whether our court order would be valid.

We were laughed at and directed to the judge in charge of bribery for that region. Through our interpreter, he explained that we could convert our American court order into a Brazilian court order, but it would be very costly and time-consuming. With the rate of our private jet, we didn't have time to waste.

The bribery judge referred us to his brother, a local lawyer who also specialized in bribery and fraudulent court orders. He requested five thousand American dollars to take the case and an additional five thousand dollars for rush service and fifteen thousand in expenses for his brother to hear our case. At the proceeding, the only ones present were the father, my investigator, the attorney, the judge, and me.

It took less than ten minutes. The attorney pleaded our case for the judge, who decided to grant us custody of the children and allowed us to bring the children back to the United States. He handed us a document that looked very official, had a large purple ribbon, and a large seal over the ribbon. It looked like we had won an award for bribery in Brazil.

The next step was to obtain a police permit from the local police chief. Our interpreter explained our situation to a large stocky man right out of a Raymond Chandler movie and asked for his help in getting the children back to the United States. The chief stated that he was very busy now and requested that we return next month.

Our interpreter, who obviously had received a doctorate in bribes, explained the severity of the situation with a display of pictures of dead American presidents worth one thousand dollars.

The chief apologized for not realizing the severity of the situation and assigned two of his best men to enforce our local court order. They charged us a transportation fee of one hundred dollars for riding in an official vehicle—the best bargain we had found in Brazil so far.

We arrived at the house and found the mother highly intoxicated. She flailed at us, screaming obscenities in at least two slurred languages. As for the children, we found them in the back of the home with a housekeeper. The woman told our interpreter that it would be best if the children went with their father as the mother was abusive to the children and didn't care for them. She also advised us that the children's mother was having an affair with a local politician and that if she called him, he would make sure that we landed in a Brazilian jail.

We cut the phone lines going to the home. The mother, who was handcuffed by the police, started running down the dirt driveway, yelling and screaming that we were stealing her babies. The local police stopped her before she had a chance to have the whole town set up as a lynch mob.

We thought that we had to get the children back to the plane as quickly as possible. We had taken our walkie-talkies with us and left a set with the pilots to let them know when to get the plane ready. However, the walkie-talkies didn't work. We were too far from the plane to reach the pilots.

The local police placed the children into a police car and we departed toward the airport, sirens screaming. When we were about two miles from the airport, we were able to reach the pilots, who assured us that they would be ready by the time we reached the airport. We had landed at a private air strip that wasn't regulated by any air traffic control.

We approached the plane just as the pilots had readied the aircraft for departure. As we turned around, we saw a group of federal police officers in hot pursuit. Since we were out of bribe money, we felt it would be in our best interests to leave the federal police behind and maybe start a pen-pal relationship once we reached the safety of our home country.

We taxied down the runway just as the federal police arrived, and were off the ground in a matter of seconds. The children wept with joy as we banked left and headed northwest back to Los Angeles. They hugged their daddy and told him how much they missed him.

Their mother had lied to the children and said their father had died in an automobile crash. The bereaved children were told that they would have to live with their mom far away so they wouldn't be put into a home for orphans. As bad as their life was living in Brazil with an alcoholic abusive mother, they figured it was better than an orphanage.

The children, now adults, were successfully raised to maturity by a father who remarried and a stepmother who loved them. They all received professional therapy regarding their experiences in Brazil.

Most kidnapped children have been abducted by a parent who lost a custody battle. Even though they have no legal rights to the child, they are angry and frustrated, and often want to hurt their ex-spouse.

You have one major thing in your favor: these abductors don't know how to hide. They may change their name, but they normally don't change their social security number. A simple social security number check will reveal their new address and new name. If that doesn't work, run a credit report and see if they are paying their bills.

If you know their credit card numbers, along with their social security number, driver's license numbers, old mailing address, and their mother's maiden name, you can probably find them quickly. If you know they are prone to using credit cards, have a friend call the credit card company posing as your ex. They should say that they can't find their credit card and would the credit card company mind telling them the last place that they used the card so that they could check with the place to see if they have the card?

The credit card company will ask a lot of questions. Be prepared to answer the following: the full name as it appears on the card, billing address, social security number, driver's license number, mother's maiden name, and your place of employment.

You can only do this once, so make sure your information is complete and correct. If they get suspicious, they might flag the account and you won't be able to get the information again. It normally works.

Most credit card companies are consumer friendly and will try to help you out. Don't report the card as lost. Tell them you will check to see if the card is where you last used it before making a lost or stolen report.

Most people will keep in touch with a mother, father, or friend. Call their family to see if they've heard from them, and tell them that you are preparing a police report alleging kidnapping. Advise them that you don't want anything unpleasant happening to the person, and it would be best to avoid a federal felony charge by simply calling you.

If they don't call within a month, run the phone number that you made contact with the month before to see if those people called your ex. Once you have the number, have your PI break the number and call the police with the information. Don't call the number yourself. You will tip them off and they will be on the run. Tell the police that you received an anonymous call telling you where your ex and children are, or tell them that you hired a PI through your attorney and they found them. Don't tell the police how you did it.

Not all kidnappings are by parents or grandparents. Here is one extreme case of child exploitation—a case it was my great pleasure to solve.

A widower hired a nanny to care for his nine-year-old son. He picked out a nice older woman both he and his son liked. When he returned home from work, the nanny and his son had vanished.

The police investigated, but got nowhere. That's when he called me. I tracked the woman to Mexico and not only found the boy, but at least twenty children held captive in a shack. The kids were tied together and in bad shape.

The children were soon to be auctioned off to the highest bidder. This wasn't a one-time event—these auctions unfortunately happened on a regular basis.

I called in Mexico's federal agents, and the kidnappers were quickly arrested. I not only returned the boy to his father, I personally returned the rest of the children to their distraught parents as well.

When you can't find someone through the usual means, you have to start thinking more creatively.

CHAPTER FIVE

RUNAWAYS

Most runaways contact someone from their home city or town. It is often simply a matter of finding your runaway's best friend and obtaining a copy of their phone bill. If they won't surrender it, look at the chapter on obtaining phone bills. It is probably the fastest and easiest way of finding a runaway child.

Other ways of tracking a runaway are by reviewing their phone bill from before they left and looking for clues. Most runaways will mistakenly leave some clues of what area of the country they are heading, and might even leave the phone number on a past phone bill.

You can often anticipate a child running away from home. Depression is the first danger signal. If their regular patterns have changed drastically, if they seem depressed or distant, if they lose interest in things they used to enjoy, if they suddenly become abusive or violent towards family members, if they've been getting involved with drugs, or hanging out with the wrong crowd—these are all good reasons to take your child to a physician.

If you have a child that you suspect might leave, you could take steps to discourage their actions. Get their passport and put it in your safe deposit box. Empty all of their accounts if you are a co-signer on the account. If not, report the passbook or checking account to your bank as stolen or lost. Cancel all of their credit cards. They are less likely to leave penniless. Keep all your jewelry and any other valuables in a safe or safe deposit box. Even if they aren't low enough to steal from you, they might have friends who will. Get your child into therapy and find out the reason that they want to leave.

It will take a lot of work and may also take some therapy for the family, but the time invested is worth saving a child from the horrors of living on the street and saving the parents from the emptiness, uncertainty, fear, guilt, pain, and endless nightmare of having a child run away.

We were contacted by a retired army general from Minneapolis. His thirteen-year-old daughter had been missing for two years. He wanted his daughter back. It was causing extreme hardship for the family as her mother had gone into a deep depression. The strain on the family was becoming intolerable. The police were of no help and he was becoming frustrated.

He explained to me that the reason that she had left home was she had started running with the wrong crowd, who had started her on drugs. Her family tried to get her into a detox center but she escaped and they had not heard from her since.

She would occasionally call a friend of hers back in Minneapolis, who would contact the family, telling them that their daughter was okay. But the friend would never tell them where she was; she would only let the parents know that their daughter was alive and living out her adventure.

I asked the father if the friend was friendly with the family. He assured me that she was. I asked him to get all of the phone bills that she had for the last two years and to send them to me.

After reviewing the bills, we observed a pattern of collect calls. About every two months, she would accept a collect phone call. Some people didn't realize that collect phone calls appeared on your bill along with the phone number.

We called all of the phone numbers and they were all payphones in a seedy part of Hollywood. When we made the phone calls, we would ask whoever answered the location of the payphone. If the person refused to tell us, we would call back until we found a cooperative person. Most of the calls were made from a payphone on Sunset Boulevard, an area known for young runaway sex workers.

With a picture we had received from her father, we started to work the streets, not as private investigators, but as potential tricks looking for a young sex worker. We would show her picture around, telling the young sex workers we were looking for a good time with this girl. She was known on the street as Misty.

One of the girls claimed that Misty was her ex-roommate and for a hundred bucks, she would give us her phone number and address. We made a counteroffer: for a hundred bucks, we asked her to show us where Misty lived and we would give her the money after Misty answered the phone and we verified it was her. She refused to give us Misty's home phone number and address. But for a hundred dollars, she would show us where Misty worked.

Sex workers tend to work the same streets all the time. They get to know the people in the area and feel comfortable working the same area. We were taken to a part of Sunset Boulevard called the Meat Rack, where young men and women were selling the only thing that they had left—a bit of spirit and their young bodies.

We saw Misty working a car that slowed down. A man, about sixty years old and driving a new Caddy, had stopped to chat with Misty. As we approached, the Caddy sped off. There she was, dressed in a red mini skirt, red fishnet stockings, a blonde wig, and enough makeup to cover three girls.

We approached Misty and told her we represented a client who had hired us to find her for a party. A "party" or a "date" is street lingo for a sexual experience, as most girls don't like to use words that could land them in jail.

She told us her price for a party was a hundred dollars. We claimed that the client would be coming into town in about a week. We told her we would give her fifty bucks today and another hundred when she showed up for the date. She agreed and gave us her home phone number.

We contacted her father, assuring him that his daughter was all right but that she was living as a sex worker. We set up a plan. We contacted Misty and asked her to meet us at a swanky Beverly Hills hotel at 6 p.m. the next day. We told her to take a cab and that our client would pay for it. She arrived at 6 p.m. as planned but asked for one hundred and fifty dollars. She said she was charging extra for coming to Beverly Hills. We agreed to the amount and asked her to go to room 647.

We accompanied her to the room where a man was standing with his back to us dressed in a bathrobe. As he slowly turned, she realized it was her father. He had tears in his eyes when he saw the way his daughter was dressed. Her initial reaction was anger but quickly changed to tears as she embraced her father. They left town the next day to return to Minneapolis.

Misty returned home and became Marsha again. She completed high school, and went on to college. We receive letters every so often from the general updating us on Marsha's progress. We eventually received a letter letting us know he had become a grandfather. He sent along a picture of Marsha, her husband, and little Ruth, their baby daughter.

I doubt her husband knows, or would ever believe, that his charming wife was once a teenage sex worker on the streets of Los Angeles. There is no reason for him to know and no reason for her to tell. Whatever skills she acquired on the job are to his benefit, and if she works outside the home, she needn't include this freelance activity on her résumé.

Chapter Six

How Businesses Get Screwed

The biggest problem facing American business is "shrinkage." The word *shrinkage* is defined as "sloppiness and theft."

If we made a pie chart of the annual multi-billion-dollar shrinkage, it would reveal that one percent is from outside burglaries and armed robberies; three percent is from breakage or spoilage; ten percent is from paperwork errors; ten to fifteen percent can be attributed to shoplifters; and approximately seventy-one percent is from stealing by dishonest employees.

Statistically, close to ninety percent of employees steal from their employers. I know this figure sounds outrageous, but this percentage doesn't include only those who embezzle large sums of money, but those who take little things such as pens and stationary.

If ninety percent of potential employees are going to steal, how do you stay in business? The answer: eliminate the biggest thieves. You can live with the petty thieves. If you look at the problems caused by your employees, you will see that ninety percent of your problems are caused by ten percent of your employees. Eliminate that ten percent before you hire them, and your business' life will be healthier, happier, and longer.

We often hire employees only when we're desperate. If we are not in desperate need of employees, we seem to take more time in the interview process and become more selective in our hiring. But if we are reaching a deadline, we have a tendency to hire anyone who is not on a respirator. And more often than not, those are the employees who come back to haunt us.

CHAPTER SEVEN

THE INTERVIEW PROCESS

Most companies are fearful of losing good prospective employees. They're afraid if they take too long in the hiring process, the person will find a job elsewhere and they will lose out on a gem of an employee. This fear is unfounded. An employer should indicate that they will not hire just anyone off the street, and if a person is good enough to get in, it will be a wonderful experience working for a wonderful company.

Think about the marines' saying, "We're looking for a few good men." Their slogan used to be, "if you are good enough to get in." Let's face it. If you're breathing and can count to ten, you are good enough to get in. The slogan adds a degree of elitism to the marines.

If they said, "If you can breathe on your own and can count to ten, we want you," how many people would think of the marines as an elitist group? The answer is obvious.

Let us look at how a city hires police officers.

Step one: a written examination

Step two: an oral examination

Step three: psychological examination

Step four: physical examination

Step five: polygraph examination

Step six: drug test

Step seven: thorough background investigation

Step eight: a sixteen-week academy where they make you do things that you don't really want to do. They yell at you, intimidate you, belittle you, and, last but not least, they humiliate you.

Step nine: they put you on probation for eighteen months and put you under a magnifying glass for the entire time. You are given a partner whose job is to train you or to get you to quit.

Then they let you become a police officer, place you in an atmosphere devoid of ethics or honesty, corrupted by politics and crime, where your life is in danger from criminals and/or fellow police officers. And yes, the pay sucks. A good cop is the next best thing to an angel from heaven; a bad cop can make your life hell. I know—I was a cop.

For every police officer job that opened up in the United States a few decades ago, there were up to three hundred applicants. By 2023, the situation was far different. Police departments were having fewer applicants than ever before. The once pervasive glamor factor of being a cop had significantly dimmed.

Perhaps a career in law enforcement seemed glamorous on TV and in the movies. In real life, there isn't any glamour at all. Whatever you do for a living, or whatever type of business you have, I assure you that it is more glamorous than being a cop.

Chapter Eight

The Wrong Way to Deal With Employees

When an applicant shows interest in becoming an employee, here is what some companies do.

1. Tell the applicant about the company.
2. Ask the applicant what they know of the company.
3. Realize the applicant will be lying about their past.
4. Lie to the applicant about how great the job is, make up benefits that don't exist, and tell them about high wages for very little work.
5. Have the applicant tell you how they ran the last company they worked for and if it wasn't for them, the company would have gone under much sooner.
6. Have the applicant give you references of people who like them and will lie for them.
7. Don't check the references. Just give them an apron and put them to work.
8. When the new employee starts stealing from you, ignore it. After all, let them steal because you are paying them below minimum wage.
9. When the employee gets hurt on the job, fire them so your workman's comp doesn't go up.
10. Deduct money from their paycheck for things like union dues when there isn't really a union, use of the bathrooms, drinking coffee, etc.

11. Every chance you get, yell at the employee, telling them how stupid they are. Try to do this in front of other employees in case they were going to try something stupid.

There are many—too many—other things that a company can do to increase their turnover and ruin morale. Most companies already know all of the wrong things to do. It is reflected in their profit and loss statements.

A DISHONEST EMPLOYEE

Bud seemed like just another average teenage guy. He had never been in serious trouble. One summer, he got a job in a sporting goods store. After working there for three weeks, Bud noticed that the assistant manager was giving skis and clothing away to his friends. It sure looked easy. When he approached the assistant manager to ask what the store policy was on employee discounts, the assistant manager said the policy was to take what you can but don't get caught.

Bud thought this was a great policy and immediately started participating in this most generous offer. The first thing he did was steal a t-shirt by stuffing it down his pants in the men's room. He walked out of the store with the rest of the employees at quitting time and didn't get caught. He thought that this was great and easy too.

As time went on, Bud became a little more adventurous and figured out how to steal cash from the register without getting caught. He would just fail to record sales. Let's say a customer was in the store and wanted to buy a sweater that cost forty-nine dollars and the customer was paying cash. All Bud had to do was put the money in the cash register and not ring up the sale. At the end of the night when he counted out the register, he would be forty-nine dollars over.

Bud realized the company checked overs and shortages, so he would steal the forty-nine bucks and the register would come out perfect. No overs or shortages. Perfect.

Bud was getting ingenious in his approaches to theft. He figured out how to let his friends steal from the store. After working there a very short time, his friends started asking if they could get a discount.

Bud told all of his friends of the most liberal discount policy he had ever seen and he was soon inundated with friends. All of the kids at school had heard about this great policy and were taking advantage of Bud's newfound wealth.

His friends would enter the store. When Bud was on the register, they would purchase an item for two or three bucks. Bud, being the ingenious person that he was, would fill the bags with merchandise, ring up three dollars, and his friends would walk out of the store with up to five hundred dollars in products and clothing.

Some of his friends wanted a lot more merchandise than they could carry out. So Bud had some more ingenious plans. Late at night, Bud would take out the trash. These trash bags were filled with merchandise. He would give these to waiting friends, who would load their cars, and eventually trucks, with the stolen goods. But that soon became blasé for Bud because it was too much work.

Bud soon became the assistant manager after his mentor went on to bigger and better things. He now had the keys to the store and had the responsibility of locking up and opening up in the morning. For this, he received an extra twenty cents an hour. Bud had great ideas now that he was in management.

The first thing that he did was have a midnight party in the store. He invited all of his newfound friends. Bud opened the store at midnight and let all of his friends into the store for a free-for-all. That night, the store lost over twelve thousand dollars in merchandise. After his friends took what they wanted, Bud was a hit.

He could also open the store early in the day. He would open early so his friends who had to work at night could get their fair share. Other mall employees had a similar deal going with their fellow mall employees. They would let employees from other stores steal whatever they wanted in return for the same privilege. By this time, Bud had gotten into cocaine, when one of the mall employees invited him to a party and told him that he should be trading merchandise for drugs, not just giving it away.

Bud started trading store merchandise in return for seventy-five bucks in coke per day. He was also stealing from customers by overcharging on items. If questioned, he would apologize and re-ring the sale.

This was also too much work. So he came up with another idea: fictitious overcharges and refunds. He would keep the customer's receipt and when they left, he would say it was a return. After getting someone's name and address out of the phonebook, he would write a phony refund or take the receipt and write it up as a sale that was rung incorrectly. Then he would steal the money.

After six months of unchecked theft, Bud's world quickly came to an end when the company scheduled his store for an inventory. A group of auditors came into the store and started counting all the merchandise in the store, along with auditing Bud's paperwork.

Bud thought he wouldn't get caught and continued his theft of cash, thinking the cash wouldn't show up as a loss in the inventory. The auditors completed their audit, showing ninety-three thousand dollars in shrinkage over the last six months. They turned the figures over to the security department, who installed a closed-circuit video system in the store. They hid the cameras in vents and sprinkler heads and waited for the first fish to bite. It didn't take very long before half the employees in the store were captured on videotape.

When the store investigators entered with the local police, terror rang out in the mall as nine employees were marched out of the store in handcuffs and arrested for grand theft, embezzlement, and conspiracy to commit a felony. All nine were minors so their parents had to be notified.

Five of the parents obtained attorneys and four parents didn't pick up their children from the police station and refused to post bail. Bud's family had an attorney and had him out of jail in less than two hours. He told them how other employees were stealing from the store but claimed he was not involved. He even lied to his attorney, claiming he had never stolen from the store.

On the day of the trial, Bud's parents were already contemplating a lawsuit against the store for false arrest, illegal detention, and mental cruelty until the videotapes were introduced as evidence, showing their son stealing cash and merchandise on a wholesale level.

They all pled guilty to misdemeanor grand theft, received three years probation, and had to make full restitution to the store.

Bud was still hooked on coke. His habit had gone from seventy-five dollars a day to three hundred dollars a day in freebase. When he approached his friends to help pay off his part of the loss, they refused to talk to him. His parents had to get a second mortgage on their home to pay off Bud's part of the bill.

CHAPTER NINE

HIRING EMPLOYEES

There are some successful companies that seem to have low turnover and also get high-quality employees with little problems. I didn't say "problem free," just fewer problems. This is how they do it.

THE WAY WE SUGGEST OUR CLIENTS HIRE

1. Interview the employee as you would talk to a friend. Remove the employer/employee barrier. Don't act as a boss. Let the employee talk and ask questions. Look over the application, but don't have it in your hand while interviewing. Don't take notes as the applicant talks. If you can, go out for a walk with the applicant, away from your phone and any interruptions. Never interview behind a desk. It works as a barrier between you and the applicant.

Find a common ground. "Oh, you were born in New York? So was I." Compliment the applicant. "My, that is an attractive ring you are wearing. Is it an emerald?" Ask the applicant what type of things they like to do on their time off. What kind of hobbies do they enjoy. It is illegal to ask someone's age, but it can be figured out very easily by deducting eighteen years from the year they graduated high school. As an example, if someone graduated high school in 1964, deducting eighteen years from the year 1964 gives the year of birth.

2. Look for problems. For example: gaps in employment that can't be explained, job hopping, problems with previous employers, or personality conflicts with past employers or employees.

3. When conducting a background check on a prospective employee, don't ascribe a lot of credibility to references. Prospective employees will normally put down references they know will give them a good recommendation.

Test the reference by asking trick questions. For example: "It shows here that before John worked for you, he worked for the ABC Company in San Francisco as a manager. Does the application he filled out for you reflect that?"

If you are asking a trick question, like making up the ABC Company as a previous employer, and the reference confirms the information, you will realize the person that you are talking to is a phony and can't be trusted to give an accurate reference.

4. Tell the employee when your hiring process is rather involved—there is the first interview and then a security company will conduct an extensive background investigation.

5. Ask if there is anything in their past that might disqualify them for employment with the company. Tell them that something they think will disqualify them might not. For example, if they shoplifted as a child, you wouldn't turn them down for that. But if they were a paid assassin, that would be a different story.

6. Ask if there is something they would like to discuss with you before setting up the appointment? Give the employee a chance to disqualify themselves before you go any further. If they don't balk at this, tell them that your company is

very selective in its interview and hiring process and that you only accept the most qualified persons. Normally, you submit three or four people for the same job and only contact the person who is the most qualified. Tell them after the security interview, there will be a drug test and a physical examination.

7. Ask if there is any part of your hiring process that they might have difficulty with? Once again, give them a chance to bow out gracefully. The last step of our hiring procedure is an interview with the boss. The application procedure should take about three days. Ask if this is okay with them.

If they are willing to go through that, chances are that you have someone who wants to work for your company. If you turn them down anywhere in the process, send them a letter thanking them for their application with your company but unfortunately, there was someone who was a better fit for the position.

Not all employer/employee relationships are exemplary. Some are downright dangerous, demented, and decidedly illegal.

CHAPTER TEN

WHEN SOMEONE HARASSES YOU

We were hired to find an ex-employee who had been sending anti-Semitic hate mail to his former boss. The threats were increasing, and the police were unable to find the person.

All of the information we were given about this ex-employee, except for his name, was fictitious. His social security number, home address, references, and date of birth were all fake. It was a difficult case. The phone number he had given the store was disconnected and there was no new number.

After interviewing some of the employees in the store, it was established that this ex-employee, whom we will call Ollie, was a student at a community college in the San Francisco area. That was the only lead we had.

My first call was to the Community College of San Francisco. Here is how the conversation went.

"Community College of San Francisco."

"May I have the admissions office, please?"

"I will connect you."

"Hello, this is Rob, admissions."

"Hi, Rob," I said, "this is James from Cal State Admissions."

"Hi, James, how are you doing today in L.A.?"

"Oh, you know how it goes—work, work, work. Never any time for fun anymore, but it's still better than when I was doing those old Soloflex TV Commercials."

"You did Soloflex commercials?" He laughed.

"Yes, but it wasn't as glamorous as you might think—unless you call sweating under hot lights in skimpy shorts glamorous. This is more stable and I can allow my rear to get as wide as I want."

Thoroughly amused, Rob offered to give me whatever I wanted. "What can I do for you today?"

"Well," I said, "have a request for transcripts from one of your students and we sent them and they were returned to us, address unknown. Could you help me by looking up his address for me? Do you need my CDE number?"

"CDE number? What is that?"

"My California Department of Education number. It's 4086. Oh, I forgot. CDE numbers are only used by state universities to identify ourselves when we make a phone call, so you know it really is a university calling." There is really no such thing as a CDE number.

"I don't need your number, James. I wouldn't know what to do with it."

Rob came back to the phone with the subject's real name, date of birth, social security number, California driver's license number, his family's address, the classes that he attended, a new address, and a new phone number. Capturing the wannabe Nazi was now remarkably easy.

If Rob is reading this, I confess that I wouldn't know a Soloflex machine if it bit me on the bottom, and I wouldn't know a sit-up from a bench press, but thanks for the information.

CHAPTER ELEVEN

FINDING BIRTH PARENTS

My television show, *Case Closed*, ran for several years on the USA Network. Prior to selling it to USA, I pitched it to Robert Uncle, an executive at Fox. In turn, he put me in contact with the producers of a series called *Families*.

The production company was looking for a girl's birth parents. They had given her up for adoption at birth. The production company had tried two other investigators, who had both come up with the wrong people. All we had to work with was a birth certificate, which we found out was fictitious. The birth parents listed on the birth certificate were not real.

The woman had made up a name for herself and we weren't sure if the man's name was real or made up. It was going to be a difficult case. I quoted the production company a price on a guaranteed basis. If I found them, they would pay my fee. If I did not, there would be no charge. It was a stupid deal. I had no idea how much work I would have to put into this case. It is hard enough to find birth parents when you have their true names. But working with phony names is quite a task. The other investigator had worked the case for months to no avail.

If other investigators took months to find the wrong people, I would find the right people in a week. I became obsessed with the case. But the harder we worked, the farther away we got from finding the birth parents.

This is all we had to work with:

Child name: *First, Middle, Last* Sanders
Place of birth: Denver
Date of birth: May 13, 1958
Sex: Female
Name of hospital
1001 Jasmine Street
City or town: Littleton
Birth Father: Talbot, Richard Lee
Color: White
Age: 20
Birthplace: New Jersey
Occupation: A/30
Kind of business: USAF
Mother: Laura Jean Sanders
Color: white
Age: 21
Mother's Marital Status: Single
Birthplace: Colorado
Address: 911 South Prince Street, Littleton, Colorado
Colorado General Hospital
Date Signed: May 13, 1958
Date Received: June 12, 1958
Registers Signature: Unintelligible
State of Colorado, United States of America

We found out that the hospital no longer existed. All of the records were given to the Salvation Army. We found that there was no Laura Jean Sanders born in Colorado twenty-one years before 1958. We checked from 1935 to 1940. However, there was a Richard Lee Talbot, born in New Jersey in approximately 1938, who was in the military in

1958. He was in the air force, stationed outside of Denver, during the time of the girl's birth. It was a start.

There were hundreds of Talbots on the East Coast during the time we were looking for a Richard Lee. We started by calling Talbots in New Jersey. After literally hundreds of calls, we found a Talbot who knew of a Talbot who, to the best of his knowledge, was in the service during 1958 and was now living in Florida.

We ran the name through a DMV source in Florida and came up with three living in Florida. We eliminated the first two by age alone: one was seventy-eight and the other was twenty-two. But one was fifty-two. We found the address through our DMV source, but there was no telephone listing for a Richard in Pompano Beach.

It was time to get creative. We ran a property check in Pompano Beach. Often, you will find a phone number listed on the property report. We found it: a phone number. Now what would we do? Call him and ask him if he had gotten a girl pregnant over thirty years ago? And if so, what was her name and did he know he had a daughter looking for him? What if he was married and never told his wife he had gotten someone pregnant over thirty years ago? It was a touchy situation. Or what if he denied it, saying he had no idea what we were talking about.

We had to come up with a gag, something that would not threaten him and make him feel guilty for not admitting he was the father. We called as a research facility looking for Laura Jean Sanders, who had given birth to a baby in 1958.

We claimed that the woman had antibodies the child needed for an operation. Even the hardest of people would give in on that one. He would not feel threatened since we were not looking for him.

We explained how Laura Jean Sanders had listed him as the birth father and would he mind helping us locate her to get her to give blood for her poor child. I choked up when relaying the story.

It turned out he was a great guy. He claimed that he did remember getting someone pregnant while in the air force, but he did not remember the name Laura Jean Sanders. He remembered first meeting the girl at a USO show in Denver. They dated for a short time, but when he found out that she was under the legal age, he stopped dating her.

"Her name," he told me, "was Linda Greenway. She looked twenty-one, but was only fourteen." He asked us to call him at work if we had any other questions and supplied us with his work number.

I can tell you exactly how many Greenways there were in Colorado from the year 1952 to the present. I have spoken to most of them. I have spent literally hours talking to Greenway families all over Colorado and so have three of my investigators. We spent over one hundred labor hours looking for Linda Greenway to no avail.

One of my investigators came up with the idea of contacting the Department of Social Services. If our subject was fourteen years old when she gave birth to a child, she might have been on state assistance at the time. We found one Greenway old enough to be Linda's mother—a Laura Greenway.

We had thought her mother's name was Maurica. We didn't see a connection but we had nothing to lose by running the social security number. It came back to Laura Greenway, 1800 South Broadway #320, Little Rock, Arkansas. I called information, holding my breath.

The number was listed.

I had to come up with a logical explanation of why I needed her daughter's new name and address. I decided on an heir search. I called her. This is how the conversation went.

Me: Mrs. Greenway?

Her: Yes.

Me: Hi, my name is John Williams and I am conducting an heir search. I am looking for a Linda Greenway, who gave birth to a daughter in May of 1958 in Colorado. Would you know of the person to whom I am referring?

Her: Why, yes. My daughter gave birth to a daughter about 1958. Goodness. How did you find me?

Me: We are calling all Greenways from coast to coast and your name was listed in the phone book as a Greenway.

Her: Well, my daughter is now living in Pennsylvania and is married to a new husband. Why again did you say you were looking for her?

Me: A man in Littleton, Colorado, passed away about six months ago and left your daughter a sum of money in his will.

Her: What was the man's name? Maybe I know him.

Me: Ralph Buccio. Did you know Mr. Buccio?

Her: No. I'm sorry. I don't know the name. How much did he leave her?

Me: Really not that much. After taxes, it comes to a little over four thousand two hundred dollars.

Her: Well, that's nice. I'm sure my daughter will be pleased with that.

Me: Would you mind helping me by giving me your daughter's name, address, and phone number? I realize she is not a Greenway anymore and I probably will never find her without your help.

Her: Why, sure.

She gave me the new name, address, and phone number. I verified the information by getting her social security number and running it through the computer. It matched her age and the time she was in Denver.

But before I go any further, I must tie up some loose ends. I called the Salvation Army, who had the records for the hospital, and asked if Linda Greenway was a patient in May of 1958. They didn't show a Linda Greenway. I asked for anyone who gave birth during the month of May who was in the home for pregnant girls during the time Laura Jean Sanders was in the home.

I received four names, addresses, and social security numbers. I found one woman who was in the hospital during the same time as our Laura Jean Sanders. She asked if the information would be kept confidential. I assured her that I would never reveal her name. She told me she remembered a Linda Greenway, whom she had known from school.

"We went to Emerson together in the 1950s," she recalled. "That's how I know her."

I called our Linda Greenway, who was now living as Linda Alkaloute in Landsdale, Pennsylvania, simply to verify the phone number and accuracy of residence.

I gave the information to the production company, who prepared to have Lisa Henery, the daughter, talk to her biological parents for the first time. They sent a production crew to my office to film the event.

I gave Lisa her father's name, along with his phone number. She placed the call. She was great. She was instructed by a group that helps adopted children find their birth parents on how to speak to her newfound parents. She was cool while the phone was ringing and then her face flushed. "Hello. My name is Lisa Henery…"

Talbot said that he believed that he was her biological father and planned to come to Los Angeles to meet her. He was great. He went on to take a DNA test to prove he was her father. They see each other on a regular basis and talk to each other on the phone.

That was one down and one to go. Then, Lisa called the ex-Linda Greenway. Linda claimed that she was not in Colorado during the time Lisa was born. We found school records to verify the fact she was there. She claimed that she was an employee in the home for unwed mothers, not a patient. We checked the social security number. She was never an employee. She went on to deny that she was Lisa's mother. She said she had her own family now and couldn't explain why her mother would say she gave birth to a child that she put up for adoption in 1958 or why another patient remembers her as a patient, not an employee. She refused Lisa's request to take a DNA test. To this day she denies being Lisa's mother.

The production company did not pay me for locating her birth mother. Despite all the evidence, they used the lack of a DNA test as an excuse to withhold payment. I should have charged them by the hour.

I believe Lisa knows in her heart that she found her birth parents. Lisa's sincere appreciation for our efforts was heartwarming—sometimes a warm heart is the best payment of all.

CHAPTER TWELVE

SO, YOU WANT TO HIDE?

A lot of people ask if it is possible to totally drop out and not be found. The answer is yes. But look at what you have to give up.

1. Change your name.
2. Change your social security number.
3. Change your driver's license.
4. Change all past addresses.
5. Never call an 800 number it appears on the caller's bill.
6. Never use your credit cards.
7. Never vote.
8. Never obtain a job that requires fingerprints.
9. Sell all of your cars.
10. Only use public transportation until you buy a car under your new identity.
11. Never call your family.
12. Never have your family call you.
13. Only use burner cell phones.
14. Sell your home.
15. Never leave a forwarding address.
16. Disconnect your phone and pay your last bill.
17. Keep a low profile.
18. Never let your picture be taken.
19. Never run for office.

20. Never go to a TV show.
21. If you are going to leave the country, you must leave from a foreign country first. Take multiple flights to your final destination, but buy your ticket when you land at the airport with no prior reservation.

Taking all of this into consideration, you must weigh the reasons why you want to hide with all the things you are about to give up.

Chapter Thirteen

Serving a Subpoena

Serving a subpoena can be a difficult task. Especially if the person you need to serve doesn't want the subpoena. Most people don't.

Rules:
1. Don't let them know you are coming.
2. Don't let them know you are coming.
3. Use every trick in this book to serve them.
4. Don't play fair.
5. Outsmart your opponent.
6. Don't let them know you are coming.

A good way of getting someone served is by investing in an inexpensive costume in order to fool a receptionist or some other protector of your intended. This can be a lot of fun, as you can see what it's like to have all sorts of different and exciting jobs. And you don't need any training or education; all you need are the right clothes.

Be a Messenger

My first suggestion is to go to a t-shirt shop that will letter t-shirts for you. Have them make up a t-shirt and have them print a name of a flower shop over the breast pocket, along with a phone number. If they are capable of other types of printing, have them make t-shirts for a messenger service, a telephone company repair service, and an express overnight delivery service. You should make up your own names, like the one I use—World Wide Courier Express.

BE A FLORIST

If you are pretending to be a floral delivery person, have a cheap arrangement of flowers and tape the subpoena on the bottom. When they least expect it, serve them. If someone stops you, tell them it must be signed for by the person receiving the flowers. If they offer to take it in for you, tell them you have to see them sign it or you will be fired. Never have the subpoena in clear sight. Always have it in an envelope or hidden away in a pocket so the person doesn't get suspicious. The messenger gag works the same way.

BE A TELEPHONE-REPAIR PERSON

The best one I've used is telephone repair. Walk in with a repair belt and a clipboard. Explain that there has been trouble reported on the line and ask where the junction box is located. Most people don't know. They will let you walk around the place unattended until you find the person you are going to serve. Walk into their office like you own the place. If anyone gives you any trouble, tell them if you leave and have to come back, there will be a seventy-five-dollar service call charge to re-book the appointment. Say that you don't know when the next available day when you can come back for a re-service would be. Explain that they have a sixty-cycle hum on their line, that their phone service may be interrupted for some time, and that they cannot hold you responsible if they don't have any phones for the next three days. People freak when they think that their business will be without phones for three days. If they are the ones responsible for not letting the repair person fix the phones, it might cost them their job. Most people will give in at this point. Tell them you have traced the trouble to your target's office and you will only be a minute. Even if he is in conference with the president, they will normally let you in for a minute, just long enough to serve him. It works.

BE A REPORTER

When I first started out in this business, every dollar counted. They still count. But today, every single dollar doesn't make the difference between success and failure.

I did an investigation for a large restaurant chain, and for reasons unexplained, they didn't pay me.

I filed a small-claims action for the money owed and gave the papers to the marshal. After trying three times, the marshal had no luck in serving any officer of the corporation. So, I had to rely on my wits.

The restaurant chain had just taken over a large ship docked in Long Beach, California. Even though I didn't do the investigation for the ship's restaurant, any officer in the corporation could be served. I ran the corporation through the secretary of state to find out the president's name.

Now, if you are a party to the action, you can't serve the papers because the courts don't trust you. They expect you to lie and say the person was served when you really didn't serve them. You must use a third party. I had a friend and a telephone and that was all I needed.

I called the corporation, posing as a reporter for *People* magazine, and was put right through. I started to interview the president over the phone. When I asked him if he would mind a picture for the article, he said, "Why, no. I wouldn't mind at all. Why don't you come over to my house this evening? I am having a party. There will be lots of celebrities and politicians there. You might even enjoy yourself."

I accepted his most generous offer and explained I would have my photographer with me. He said that would be fine and proceeded to give me directions to his home. I was a bit shocked when we arrived at the address. It was a large, gated mansion with security all over the place. We were greeted by an armed guard at the gate. My friend brought along a cheap camera, but it had a flash and looked good enough.

The armed guard asked for our names and I replied, "Oh, we are with *People* magazine," and we gave our aliases. He checked the list and, sure enough, there we were. He had to direct us to the house since one could get lost just driving up the driveway. He opened the huge security gates and we proceeded to the valet parking. We didn't really want to leave the car, as we suspected that we wouldn't be staying for dessert.

We were right. We were greeted at the door by a uniformed butler who announced our presence. I felt a little foolish as we were escorted to the host and hostess. The host came up to shake my hand. I had the camera as my friend introduced himself as the reporter. He handed our host the subpoena for small-claims court, just as our host started introducing us as reporters from *People*. Then I took his picture.

As he examined the papers, he said, "What the hell is this?" My friend told him he was being served. He turned blue right in front of our eyes. He was fuming. He said, "Get out of here while you still can."

Two plainclothes security officers escorted us out. As we left, we thanked him for his hospitality and commented that the appetizers were excellent. We were jerked by the security guards and were rushed to the door of our awaiting car. I commented to one of the security guards on the excellent valet service and asked how we should tip. We were told it would be difficult to leave if we waited much longer. We took his advice and departed.

Looking back, it was a fun time, but we sure were stupid. We could have been killed. They would still be looking for our bodies if they had decided to bury us on that long driveway. Anyway, he paid me my full amount, due the next day by messenger, along with the filing fee.

BE RICH

We were hired by a law firm to serve the VP of a large securities brokerage firm. No one was able to get this man served.

I called the VP and explained that I was referred to him by a fictitious person. I went on to tell him that my grandfather had just passed away and left me $2.3 million in his will. I asked for his help in investing this money.

There was a pause on the phone. Then he started telling me that I would be in great hands and that his track record would be hard for any other broker to beat. He said he couldn't meet with me today because he was speaking before a large group of businessmen on investing. I was impressed and asked where he was lecturing. He told me but assured me the meeting was sold out, that it had been sold out for the last three months, and that every meeting he gives is sold out way in advance. I was now really impressed.

This was the last day the subpoena could be served before the statute ran out. He had to be served by midnight. I called his secretary and, posing as the chairperson, asked if there was anything I could do to help him with the meeting. She assured me that everything would be handled by the firm. I acted like a nervous chairperson and asked her if she had the directions. She said she did and was kind enough to give them to me. For the first time, I asked her to confirm the time. She assured me that he would be there by 1 p.m. I thanked her.

I headed for the Howard Johnson's in West Covina, about thirty miles from Los Angeles. I arrived there about noon and found the meeting. I waited until about 1:45 p.m. He was on a roll as I approached the lectern as if I were going to ask him a question. I handed him the subpoena. The audience started applauding as I walked off stage, announcing that he had just been served. I can't tell you how his speech went after that, but the Kiwanis Club loved the surprise.

Chapter Fourteen

Financial Cheats

We do a lot of work involving financial dishonesty, such as catching scam artists, finding hidden assets in divorce cases, helping casinos get gambling debts paid, and locating bank accounts so people who have judgments in their favor can get paid.

The work involves finding money that people are hiding. If you receive a judgment against someone, often that is not good enough to get your money back. If people are trying to hide their money, you won't be able to get any of it. You must first find out where they are keeping the money.

FINDING HIDDEN ASSETS IN A DIVORCE CASE

We were once asked by a large law firm if we could find some hidden assets. We assured them we could and were faxed the case. This was a very interesting case. The husband was a well-known car dealer and appeared on television every day hocking his wares. He had claimed his total assets were eight hundred thousand dollars. His wife knew he had well in excess of two million but, even after reviewing the compiled CPA documents, had no idea where they were.

It seemed rather strange that about every six to eight months, he would receive a large invoice from a management company for services rendered. When we asked about this service, we couldn't get a clear explanation regarding what service this management company provided.

After a bit of research, we determined this service was in fact a bogus company set up to drain any assets that the car dealer wanted to hide.

The company came back to a Dr. Lowenthal with a PO Box in New York and no telephone number, which made it even more suspicious. We broke the PO Box to find that all the mail was being forwarded to a company in Switzerland owned by the bogus doctor.

After we looked into the company, we were more determined to break this fraud ring and recoup some of the money for our client. We contacted an associate in Switzerland and asked him to check on the address of this doctor and his management company. He knew the address as an office building in downtown Zürich set up specifically for attorneys who operated bogus companies for wealthy Americans and others with money to hide. He told us that in Switzerland, attorneys use the title "Dr." in their name because they are *Doctors-In-Law*. In the USA, we simply call them attorneys.

He went on to explain that attorneys will set up phony Swiss corporations in Zürich specifically to drain money from corporations all over the world. Because they are owned by a Swiss citizen, they receive tax benefits. He went on to explain that even though the company does exist, it doesn't mean anything because the attorney is only a figurehead and receives approximately twenty-five thousand dollars a year to afford people the right to own a company under a fictitious heading.

The attorney cannot remove any monies from the corporation, as only the person who owns the company and set it up in Switzerland can withdraw monies because they are the only ones with the account number.

In Switzerland, all you need is the account number to remove or transfer funds anywhere in the world. That is why the Swiss bank issues the number and claims no responsibility if someone gets your number and transfers funds.

Otherwise, the banks in Switzerland are pretty secure as they don't have the real name of the person the account is under. So, you must first find the phony corporation, then get the account number, and the money is yours.

Going after the doctor's records would be useless. So we focused our efforts on the husband. We had his wife go through all of his personal papers in the house, looking for anything with the doctor's name on it. After two weeks of searching, she found an address book with the doctor's name and telephone number, along with the address of his bogus Swiss corporation.

To call Switzerland from the United States, you need the overseas code, the country code, and the city code. It would look like 011-41-1-555-1212. 011 is the overseas code, 41 is Switzerland, and 1 is Zürich. This telephone number started off SF901 and a second number started off USD654. The SF was the code for Swiss francs and the USD was the code for US dollars, as you can deposit in Swiss francs or American dollars or any other currency that you choose, with a couple of exceptions.

Some countries, like South Africa, don't allow free access to your money. We had the account numbers. Now we needed the bank. There are only so many banks in Switzerland that offer numbered accounts.

On our second try, we hit pay dirt. We found a total of eleven million in a combination of Swiss francs and American dollars.

Our client transferred all but one dollar and one Swiss franc to her local bank in California. She then called the car dealer at work and asked him if he would be open to further negotiations regarding her newfound wealth.

To say that he was upset would be much like saying the *Titanic* hit an ice cube. He went crazy, telling her that the money was taxable once it hit her account. She replied that after taxes, she was still better off than what he offered as a settlement. She walked out of the marriage with a little over three million dollars.

Chapter Fifteen

Gambling Debts

We do work for the Las Vegas casinos when someone signs for credit in the form of a marker and then doesn't pay. These people will sign a marker and then close their bank account when they get home.

A marker is much like a check in that it can be processed through your checking account. The casino deposits your check or marker in their account and the bank processes the item as if it were a normal check. We find these people and their new bank accounts so that the casino can deposit the marker and get their money. This is usually fairly simple.

One particular case was different. The marker was for $204,000. We needed to find a checking account owned by that person with at least that much money in it.

The player was now a cash player and the casino didn't want to annoy him by asking for his new account number. It doesn't happen very often that the casino doesn't want to annoy you by asking for your new bank account. But when you lose $1.6 million in one night at one casino as a cash player, the casinos give you a little leeway on your past debts.

As it was explained to me one day in one of the biggest casinos in Las Vegas, if someone loses half a million dollars in one night and bounces a marker for fifty thousand, so what? What did it cost the casino, a free room and meals?

Their overhead remained the same and they are still up four hundred fifty thousand dollars for the price of a suite and some meals. Now, if you are a small gambler, and you owe the casino five grand, they will collect it by turning you in to their collection department or agency. Then it is assigned to an attorney for collection. Gambling debts are legal in Nevada and you are sued under Nevada law.

I have seen people lose their homes because they got cute with a casino collection department. I wouldn't advise trying to stiff a casino unless you are a million-dollar player. But even then, they catch up to you someday. They don't stay in business by being stupid.

This player, who owed $204,000, was a Mexican citizen. This made it even more difficult. We had to find an American bank. Mexico doesn't use the ABA system of check clearing. Each bank clears its own checks. We had to find an American bank with a checking account in this player's name with at least $204,000. This was a difficult, but not impossible, task.

When we were contacted by the casino, they told us that they had assigned this case to six other investigative firms in the past and no one could find the account—or even the bank. They offered us sixty-one thousand dollars for the information.

We went to work. The first thing I did was to contact a *federale* in Mexico. He was a reliable federal police officer who had access to information in Mexico that was worth its weight in gold, or a hundred dollars, whichever was greater.

This time it was three hundred dollars. We needed phone records from our player's home phone to the United States. We hoped that in the last year, he had called his American bank.

Bingo.

An American bank was on his phone bill. Great. Now all we had to do was get the account number and we were on our way to the sixty-one thousand dollars. Not so easy. This was not your normal, friendly neighborhood bank. This was a private bank that did not belong to the FDIC and didn't have to comply with any federal regulations or insurance restrictions like a normal bank. This was a very private bank that would not release any information to anyone except the customer. Even then, the customer must provide the bank with a secret code that he made up. The code could be anything—a word, a number, or even a song.

We were stumped. I saw the sixty-one thousand dollars melting away. I called other asset investigators who may have had some luck with this bank in the past. Everyone I talked to discouraged me even more. All my predecessors had failed in the past. No one was able to get any information from this bank. It took me over one month to come up with a plan.

Here is what we did, step by step:

First, we called the subject, telling him that we were the bank. We said there was a large item being processed through his account, but before we talked to him about it, we needed his code. We told him the signature on the item didn't look like his signature and that the item was for $567,000. He told us his code name was "blue cloud" and that he wanted to talk to Victor, his banking representative. We told him that Victor was sick today and that I was the VP in charge of his account. He said that he had not written a check for $567,000 and to send it back unpaid. He asked if we could send him a copy of the check by mail. We assured him that would not be a problem and thanked him for his cooperation and courtesy regarding this matter. We also apologized for bothering him with this matter. He thanked us for calling.

We now had the code, but we still didn't have the account number or the balance. I wrote the following letter:

Dear Victor:

I had this extra money in my desk drawer. Please deposit it in my personal checking account. Please give the messenger a receipt and write down my balance. Put the receipt in the envelope and the messenger will return it to me sealed. I am on my way to the Orient, so I didn't have the time to stop in. Thank you. My code is Blue Cloud.

Signed via the signature on the marker

We made up a phony messenger pad and one of my younger investigators posed as the messenger. We had a t-shirt and a cap made up with the phony messenger's company name so he looked real. The two thousand dollars cash he had was very real.

We attached a note to the envelope, stating: "Deliver this envelope to Victor at [the bank's name, bank's address], wait for an envelope, and return to my office."

My investigator was nervous as he left the office. We had role-played every scenario before he left to make him feel comfortable with the gag. He left the office at 9 a.m. and made his way downtown.

He found the private bank in an office building on the fifth floor. The door wasn't marked. Once inside, it looked like any other lawyer's office. He showed his instructions to the girl behind the desk without uttering a word.

She took the package and instructed him to wait in the lobby. She disappeared for about eight minutes. It seemed like an eternity. She returned with an envelope that she handed to our investigator. He never spoke a word.

As soon as he had pulled out of the garage, he called the office from his car phone yelling, "I got it! I got it!" He returned to the office and handed over the goods. The envelope contained a receipt with the account number along with the balance in the account. The balance was $1,600,278.27. We all yelled out loud at the same time. We had won.

I gave the investigators who worked on the case with me a bonus of twenty-five hundred dollars each. We were all pleased, including the casino that had cashed the marker for $204,000. As far as we know, it was the first time the bank had been penetrated from the outside. I would not tell other investigators how I got the bank. I told them to read this book.

CHAPTER SIXTEEN

WHEN PEOPLE OWE YOU MONEY

We were hired to find the assets of a man who had lost a small-claims action and refused to pay someone nine hundred sixty-one dollars. We looked for any bank accounts or real property and found nothing. The client had paid us in advance for the information, so we tried our best, to no avail. I called the client to ask if he would garnish the person's wages if we got current employment. He agreed. I went to work.

Here is how the conversation went.

Me: Hello. Mrs. Smith?

Her: Yes. Who's calling?

Me: Hi. I'm Mr. Williams with the county. We're calling because Mr. Smith never returned the jury duty questionnaire and I just wanted to tell you that Mr. Smith is scheduled for jury duty on November 11. It will be at least a four-month trial and he should tell his employer.

Her: A four-month trial? My husband can't take off from work for four months. We will starve to death.

Me: Well, the next time the county sends you a jury duty questionnaire, I suggest you fill it out.

Her: We never received any questionnaire from the county. I pick up the mail and I never saw it. Honest.

Me: Do you know how many times a day I hear that one? Please.

Her: I am telling you the truth. We really never received it. Isn't there anything we can do?

Me: Well, I guess I could fill it out over the phone. Let's say it would be a hardship on your family for your husband to leave for four months. Would that be true?

Her: Yes, yes. It would be true.

Me: Okay. Is your husband currently employed? And where does he work? And what is the phone number where we can verify this information?

She gladly answered all of my questions... and I gave her a six-month deferment from jury duty for being so nice over the phone.

My client collected his judgment, and I my fee.

CHAPTER SEVENTEEN

MORE HIDDEN ASSETS

We were contacted by an investigator who had a case she couldn't crack. Her client had received a judgment in the amount of one hundred thousand dollars against a sadomasochism club. The client had invested monies into the club and the owner refused to repay the money or even to let the investor see the books.

As embarrassed as he was about suing the club, he went ahead and won his judgment. The problem was collecting the monies. The club had drained all of its accounts after the judgment.

We thought one of our investigators could join the club and when their check cleared the bank, we would have their account number. Not so easy. The club had six locations but was not taking any new members.

Now, remember, some of the people who would join this type of club would want to be belittled and talked down to. I didn't take this into consideration when I called the club regarding membership. Here is how the conversation went.

Me: Hello. I am interested in joining your club. Can you tell me how to go about it?

A man's voice on the phone: Who the fuck are you? Do we know you? We don't take every jerkoff who calls us. We've been in business for over five years and if it took that long for you to find us, you are not the kind of person we want to join our club. We have the cream of the crop here and you sound like some type of jerk-off. We don't want you.

Click. He hung up on me. I dialed the phone again.

Me: Hi. I just called and I was wondering if any of your members ever sell their memberships and would sell for five hundred or a thousand dollars?
Voice: Five hundred or a thousand bucks? We have people here who will spend one hundred thousand per year to come and live out their lifelong fantasies. You are more of a dumb jerk-off than I thought you were. Don't bother me, you asshole. Lose my number, you jerkoff.
Me: Wait a second. Stewart Page gave me your phone number. Does that help?
Voice: Who the fuck is Stewart Page? Any asshole can call up and make up a name. Are you out of your fucking mind? The top mistresses in the business refer their clients to us, and they pay through the fucking nose to stay members. Who knows you? Have a member come to me and vouch for you, show me your net worth, and if you're worth talking to, I might consider a membership. But don't get your hopes up, you lowlife motherfucker. You are probably some asshole that doesn't deserve to wipe their ass at our club. Lose my number, jerkoff.

Obviously, I wasn't speaking to Dale Carnegie, nor was this the customer relations employee of the year. After thinking about the way I was treated, if I were into humiliation, it was perfect for someone who would join this type of club in the first place.

This was a tough one. I had some of my female operatives try to call for a job, but they were all shot down quickly for lack of experience and a lack of clientele. I had to find someone who was into this type of behavior and get them in on the inside to find the bank accounts.

I searched the sex ads in a local publication that had those types of readers and came up with a woman who called herself a mistress of domination. She was open to earning some extra cash for some investigative work.

I met her at her home in the Hollywood Hills. It was scary to see all of the implements she had to have to be in the business: racks, leather, rubber, whips, and, of course, some chains. She was a woman in her late thirties, about five feet, ten inches tall, and weighed about one hundred thirty-five pounds. She had black hair and dark brown eyes. She charged me a two-hundred-fifty-dollar consultation fee. She claimed it was standard in her business. After all, she was selling time and information.

I asked her if she knew of the club and she told me she had, but the reason she didn't take her clients there was their percentage was too high. She claimed that she was a former sex worker, but since the HIV epidemic, this business was much safer since it didn't require any sex.

According to her, it was not illegal to whip someone for money. She asked for five thousand dollars to help me with the case, and we split the difference. She agreed to turn over all account information to us. In return, we agreed never to tell anyone her name or that she helped us obtain this information.

Within two days, she had given us four accounts at four separate banks, totaling over one hundred sixty thousand dollars. Our client attached the accounts and added the cost of our investigation. The total recovered, including all fees, was $136,567.96. The club wasn't pleased, but our client was thrilled.

I once again called the club.

Me: Hello. Are you accepting new members?
Voice: Why, yes. We are. How were you referred to us?

Me: By the jerk-off who just emptied your accounts, you idiot.

Voice: Who is this? I will get you, you son of a bitch.

I hung up the phone.

CHAPTER EIGHTEEN

PROTECTING YOUR PRIVACY

IT'S HARD TO KNOW WHO TO TRUST

There so much dishonesty today that it's hard to know whom you can trust. Everywhere you turn, someone is ready to take advantage of you. Just look at Bob and Mary as they prepare to go out for the evening.

Bob and Mary hire a neighborhood teenager, let's call her Judy, to watch their children. Judy has been babysitting for Bob and Mary for two years without a problem. However, this night, Judy will call her teenage boyfriend, Roy, the minute Bob and Mary walk out the door.

Roy has always liked Judy and takes her up on it, arriving only minutes after Bob and Mary leave. While Judy is checking on the children, Roy excuses himself to go to the bathroom. He goes to Bob and Mary's bedroom, where he quickly goes through the closets and drawers in hopes of finding some type of treasure he can pawn for his rather expensive drug habit.

It is not very long before he finds Bob's gun and coin collection, which he puts in a pillowcase and throws out of the bedroom window to be picked up later.

Bob and Mary arrive at the restaurant and surrender their car to the valet, who gives them a ticket for their car. They sit down to a wonderful meal. After coffee and dessert, Bob asks for the check but doesn't look at it. He just leaves the cash and doesn't wait for his receipt. What Bob doesn't realize is that the waiter has given Bob a different table's check, which is thirty dollars more than his check. The waiter will then pocket the difference after he gives the same check to the party who had ordered the more expensive meal.

Bob also didn't realize that while they were waiting for their table at the bar, the bartender never gave them a receipt and put the cash Bob left in his tip cup.

As Bob and Mary exit the restaurant, the busboy starts clearing the table, along with the cash Bob had left for the bill and the twenty percent tip for the waiter. Bob is stopped at the door by the manager asking Bob if he intends to pay for dinner. Bob is angered by the insinuation that he would walk out on a check and walks the manager back to the table to show that he indeed left the money for the check.

Upon returning to the table, he realizes the table has been cleared, along with the money he left. Bob asks the busboy to tell the manager that he left sixty-five dollars in cash on the table. The busboy looks at Bob with a blank stare, not having a clue what Bob is talking about.

Bob orders the busboy to empty his pockets, which the busboy does without hesitation, as he had handed off Bob's money to the dishwasher long ago. Bob finds only some loose change in the busboy's pocket. Embarrassed and humiliated, Bob hands the manager a credit card and pays the same bill twice, this time leaving the waiter only a fifteen percent tip.

As they leave the restaurant red-faced, they look for the valet but he is nowhere to be found. Bob re-enters the restaurant, ticket in hand, looking for the manager. The manager has heard enough for one night. Bob shows the manager the valet parking ticket, with the number twenty-five written in crayon, and asks for the valet. The manager explains to Bob that they do not offer valet parking and has no idea where Bob received this colored paper with the number written in crayon.

As Bob calls the police to report his car stolen. Mary calls Judy to make sure the kids are okay. After speaking to Judy, Mary feels relieved to know at least the children are okay.

They arrive home in a taxi cab at 1 a.m. to find Judy sleeping on the couch, naked with Roy. Both of them are so drugged up, they don't realize that Bob and Mary have returned. Bob pays Judy and asks them both to leave while Mary checks on the children.

They get into bed around 1:45 a.m. Roy hides on the side of the house until he sees the light go off. Then he grabs his stash outside the window and heads for the local drug dealer to cash in Bob's possessions. It turned out to be quite an expensive night for Bob and Mary.

Three days later, Bob finds the theft of his gun and coin collection. He decides not to start trouble and puts in a claim to his insurance company for the loss. But Bob had never declared his coin collection, so Bob receives a check (minus his deductible) for $2.57.

CHAPTER NINETEEN

HOW TO AVOID BEING FOOLED BY A PI

The number one way a private investigator will get information about you is not from the Department of Motor Vehicles or from a credit reporting agency. The fastest and easiest way to get information from someone is from the person themselves. Oh, I know that you would never give information to a stranger. But let me paint you a picture of how information is given out to investigators on a daily basis. The first thing they do is run your credit. Let us say that you have creditors who are not exactly happy with you. Let us say that your monthly bills outweigh your income substantially. Here is what happens.

PI: Hello, is this Mrs. Jones?

Mrs. Jones: Yes, who is calling?

PI: My name is Bob Jones from Visa/Mastercard processing center and the reason that I am calling today is to offer you a Visa or Mastercard that has been pre-approved by your bank.

Mrs. Jones: Really? How much is this going to cost me? How much do I have to put down?

PI: Put down? Nothing. Since you have been pre-approved, we will waive the membership fees the first year just to get you as a member. You know all the competition that is out there with American Express and Discover Card?

Well, this is our way of getting new members and if you are willing to make an application today, we will waive the regular eighteen percent interest fee on unpaid balances for the first year and charge you a preferred rate of ten percent per year on the unpaid balance. Can I get you to fill out the application now right over the phone?

Mrs. Jones: What information do you need?

PI: Well, first let me verify your social security number. Is it 123-45-6789?

Mrs. Jones: Yes, it is.

PI: And do you live at 123 Elm Street, Anywhere, USA?

Mrs. Jones: Why, yes, I do.

PI: Okay. Now, I just need your current employment.

Mrs. Jones: I work for ABC Company as a supervisor.

PI: And Mr. Jones? Where is he employed?

Mrs. Jones: He is a truck driver for the ABC Company.

PI: And your monthly income?

Mrs. Jones: I make one thousand two hundred dollars a month.

PI: And Mr. Jones? His monthly income?

Mrs. Jones: He makes two thousand dollars a month.

PI: And bank references? Where do you presently maintain accounts? I need all checking, saving, CDs, and all your stocks, bonds, and securities.

Mrs. Jones: We have a checking account and savings account at the OK Bank and Loan. Our account numbers are 12333455667 and 555666777888. We don't have any CDs but we do have an account at Better Stock Company, where we have two thousand shares of MBI that my husband's grandfather left to him in his will. And we have a car that is paid off and I have my wedding ring that is worth four thousand dollars, or so my husband says. You see, I can't always believe him. He was in the hospital for a while because of his drinking. Anyway, we got behind in our bills and my sister had to loan us money. Anyway, we borrowed three thousand dollars so they wouldn't take our house away from us…

Sometimes it is hard to stop them once they get on a roll. Mrs. Jones would tell the PI the most intimate details of her sex life at this point. She finally has someone who will listen to her and she can't wait to unload all of her family secrets to a total stranger.

If we were to call Mrs. Jones and tell her we needed information so that our client can collect their money, we wouldn't get very far. This story shows only one type of scenario of the hundreds that are used on a daily basis by PI firms all over the world. It is our way of obtaining information.

CHAPTER TWENTY

EVEN WALLS CAN HAVE EYES AND EARS

The people private investigators investigate are, for the most part, people who either owe money or refuse to pay or are wanted criminals. Sometimes, however, innocent people have their privacy invaded.

Sometimes there is not much you can do to protect yourself from these people. But if you are aware that these things happen, you can learn to be suspicious in certain situations.

We were contacted by clients who were on vacation. They had been driving up the California coast and had stopped for the night at a quaint old hotel run by an older couple. They checked in at approximately 6 p.m. They got a well-decorated, comfortable room that had antiques and a large bed with a handmade comforter. They went out for dinner and returned to their room at about 9 p.m.

They were looking for an ice machine when they walked into an office where a group of men were sitting around a television watching some X-rated videos. One of the men approached the couple and asked them if he could be of any help. They asked about the location of the ice machine. The room clerk advised them that it was in the kitchen and that he would get them the ice they needed.

As the clerk left the office area, the couple noticed that, although the volume was turned down, the room in the

X-rated movie looked familiar. They didn't say anything until they headed back to the room. They asked each other if the other had noticed a resemblance to their room in the X-rated video.

Their first thought was that the hotel rented out their rooms for X-rated videos. The one thing that didn't seem right was that the camera in the video didn't move—a hidden camera was filming guests having sex. They immediately checked out.

The next day, they hired us to conduct an investigation into the hotel to find out if the hotel indeed had secret video cameras in the room.

Once finding out the room number, we made reservations at the hotel. We requested the specific room, claiming that it was our anniversary and that we stayed in that room on our honeymoon night.

They confirmed our reservations and a male and female operative checked into the room. Their bags had electronic equipment to detect any video or audio transmissions coming from the room. They quickly found a camera hidden in the air vent and a microphone hidden behind a picture.

They disconnected the camera, cut the microphone cable, and quickly left the hotel. They filed a police report and helped the police conduct a raid on the hotel. They found over one thousand five hundred videotapes of guests having sex, tapes the motel was selling to the general public.

After arresting all employees and the owners, the police confiscated the hotel records to contact all the innocent couples who had been violated. The couples got together and with the help of an attorney, received a judgment in the amount of fifteen million dollars. They forced the sale of the hotel and its property and forced the owners into bankruptcy after collecting over three million dollars in revenues the owners had made from the sale of the videos.

CHAPTER TWENTY-ONE

GARBAGE

People don't realize how much others can find out about them from their garbage. Trash is a literal storehouse of information. Take it from a veteran trash investigator. Here are things that I have found in the trash:

- Cash receipts
- Phone bills
- Employee records
- Tax records
- Canceled checks
- Credit card statements
- Social security numbers
- PIN codes for money machines
- Codes for computer entry
- Prescriptions with the subject's name and other names that proved to be helpful in our investigation
- Bottles of expensive wine with fingerprints
- Bottles of cheap liquor with fingerprints
- Company bids
- Old invoices with the customer's name, address, and phone number
- Lewd pictures
- Non-lewd pictures
- Pictures that later turned into evidence
- Murder weapons

- Taped phone conversations
- Audio tapes to friends
- Audio tapes from friends
- Videotapes to and from friends
- Lewd videotapes
- Illegal videotapes of crimes
- Drug paraphernalia
- Drug packaging
- Daily employee kitty sheets to keep count of what has been stolen in cash
- Baby diapers from someone who claims to be single without children
- Matchbooks from restaurants
- Lipstick-stained cigarettes
- A lot of old smelly food and coffee grounds

This list is just a partial list of treasures that can be found in someone's trash. Here is the Wolfson technique for obtaining and sorting trash.

First, you have to get the trash. This may not be an easy task since in some cities, like L.A., the trash still belongs to a person until it gets to the dump, even though the trash is at the curb. But most cities do not have an ordinance regarding trash. The reason that L.A. put this trash rule on the books is to prevent people from going through your trash, taking out recyclables to sell, and then leaving the rest of your trash in the street.

So, if you're in L.A., you can still get that treasured trash. Here is the way we do it. We wait for garbage day. When the trash is placed at the curb, we mark the trash with fluorescent paint for later identification. Or we may hand some pictures of dead presidents to the trash man to place it in our vehicle.

I would suggest wearing old clothes and if you are approached, grumble something unintelligible as if you were a street person just picking up trash and looking for something to eat. They might even invite you into their house for a snack. Stranger things have happened.

Let us assume that the city that you live in doesn't have any laws regarding trash pick-up. The first thing that you must do is find out what day the trash is picked up. Some cities will post it on a sign, prohibiting you from parking on a certain side of the street on trash day. If there are no signs, drive through the neighborhood for a few nights and see what day the trash is placed by the curb.

Now we have the trash. What do we do next? First, we are going to buy rubber gloves and aprons before going through it. I would also suggest a face mask. It will help protect you from catching any communicable diseases. The next thing we do is, we go piece by piece through the trash. We unfold each small piece of paper; look at each matchbook; examine every item for clues or for something that might prove incriminating. Don't overlook anything. The smallest scrap of paper may contain the phone number that you have been looking for.

You're thinking how easy it is to poke through people's garbage. Let me explain some setbacks. Here are some of the downsides to trash collecting:

- High-rise apartment building trash is usually all mixed in together, so one must stand by the trash shoot.
- You can find things like maggots crawling around someone's trash.
- Roaches are a way of life for a trash investigator.
- You may find disease-contaminated needles.
- You may find dead babies or severed body parts.

But remember, once your trash hits the streets, it is fair game and any conman or PI can obtain information on you.

Chapter Twenty-Two

Rules For Protecting Your Privacy

Investigators rely on three things: their wits, their contacts, and their subject's trash. With these three things, there isn't anything that they can't find out about someone. But if you take the following precautions, you can foil even the most seasoned private investigator.

Don't give any information to anyone over the phone without a callback number which you can use to verify they are who they say they are. After you get the callback number, call information to verify the number before calling them back.

Preferably, I would rather see you get the information in the mail. If they don't have your address, don't give it to them. Don't give out any information over the phone without a callback number. I don't care if it is the police department—ask for a callback number. If it is really the police, they won't mind giving you a callback number. So, our first rule is: no information over the phone without a callback number.

Don't give any information to someone who shows up at your house taking a survey, who offers to give you a free termite inspection, or any other guise that PIs and sometimes burglars use. Just don't tell anyone anything personal about your life. Sometimes they start off very innocently. Then, before you know it, they have your credit card numbers and expiration dates.

No information to strangers unless you can verify who they are. As an example, if someone tells you they are taking the census, ask for proof that they are really census takers before you give any information.

Get a mail drop. A mail drop is a private mailbox that is not under the supervision of the federal government. It appears as a normal address and an apartment or unit number. Use this mail drop for everything: your driver's license, all subscriptions to magazines, all of your utility bills, your phone bill, and credit card applications. Use this address as your home address.

For a home phone number, use an answering service that answers calls by phone number or that just says "hello." Instruct the answering service to forward messages to your home phone. Also, tell the service that your ex-husband has been making death threats and not to give out your home number to anyone. As far as they are concerned, they are your roommate. And send this to them in writing and have them post it above your number or on their computer. They should not give any information to anyone. Give them a neighbor's phone number to be used in case of an emergency if they have to get a hold of you.

Lock your trash. If you can't, don't put anything in the trash that you wouldn't want to see in the local paper, i.e., burn old credit cards, burn nude pictures that were taken by an old spouse, tear up phone bills, credit card statements, or anything else that you wouldn't want anyone to see. The *National Enquirer* goes through the stars' trash on a daily basis in hopes of finding a juicy story. If you want privacy, destroy things that are private to you.

Hire a PI to do a background on you and then plug the loopholes where they were able to get information. Call your phone company and tell them you want to flag your account. You don't want information given to anyone who calls regarding your account unless they have your code number. Assign code numbers to all your bank accounts, stocks, bonds, securities, and anyone that has any personal information on you. Assign them a code word or number.

Lock your mailbox.

Find out every time someone pulls a credit report. Credit Karma and similar services advise you when someone runs your credit.

Never cash a check from someone you don't know. This is a common way for people to get your bank account information.

If it seems too good to be true, then it is. If you receive a card in the mail telling you that you just won an all-expense-paid trip to Paris, France, and all you have to do is pay the three-dollar tax on your credit card, don't do it. It is a trick.

By now, we have provided you with plenty of tricks of your own. Every story and anecdote in this book is true, and the advice given in the final section has proven effective time after time. I suggest you take our advice to heart and apply it to your life. It could save you from financial loss and needless aggravation. If you have questions or comments send them along to us in care of Wild Blue Press.

For More News About Fred Wolfson and Burl Barer Signup For Our Newsletter:

http://wbp.bz/newsletter

Word-of-mouth is critical to an author's long-term success. If you appreciated this book please leave a review on the Amazon sales page:

http://wbp.bz/secrets

STEALING MANHATTAN

http://wbp.bz/manhattan

Edgar Award winner and New York Times bestselling author Burl Barer brings to light the remarkable story of four decades and two generations of America's First Family of kind and generous "altruistic outlaws" in STEALING MANHATTAN: The Untold Story of America's Billion Dollar Gem Heist Masterminds.

BETRAYAL IN BLUE

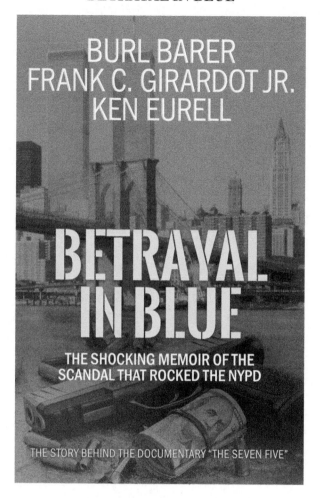

http://wbp.bz/biba

Adapted from Ken Eurell's personal memoirs of the time plus hundreds of hours of exclusive interviews with the major players, including Adam Diaz and Dori Eurell, this book reveals the truth behind the documentary *The Seven Five.*

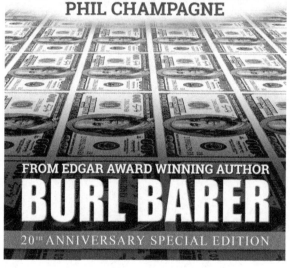

THE COUNTERFEIT RESURRECTION OF
PHIL CHAMPAGNE

FROM EDGAR AWARD WINNING AUTHOR
BURL BARER

20TH ANNIVERSARY SPECIAL EDITION

http://wbp.bz/manoverboarda

"Barer does it again! A deft and dazzling display of solid research and rapier wit—a must for all true crime aficionados."—Gary C. King, author of Love, Lies, and Murder

A TASTE FOR MURDER

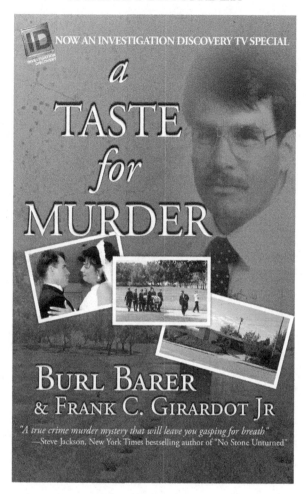

http://wbp.bz/atfma

As seen on Investigation Discovery: "A true crime murder mystery that will leave you gasping for breath." —Steve Jackson, *New York Times*–bestselling author of *No Stone Unturned*

HEADLOCK

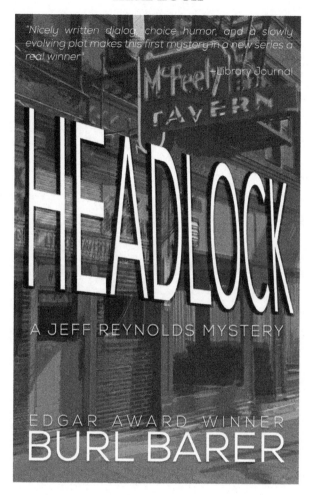

"Nicely written dialog, choice humor, and a slowly evolving plot makes this first mystery in a new series a real winner."

—Library Journal

HEADLOCK

A JEFF REYNOLDS MYSTERY

EDGAR AWARD WINNER
BURL BARER

http://wbp.bz/headlockreviews

From the New York Times–bestselling and Edgar Award–winning author Burl Barer, and featuring cameos by a few real-life mystery authors, this is a wildly entertaining PI tale in which it's hard to tell what's deception, what's delusion, and what's genuinely deadly—and all roads lead to McFeely's Tavern in Walla Walla, Washington . . .

**COMING SOON FROM JIM DUKE
AND WILDBLUE PRESS**

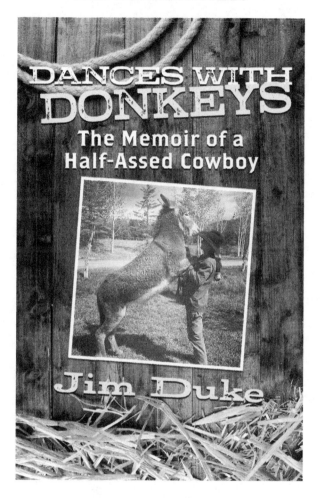

DANCES WITH DONKEYS
http://wbp.bz/donkeys

Read a sample next

Through the Looking Ass

"Why do you keep such ugly beasts,"
it's often asked of me.
"Why not have one horse at least,
so beautiful, wild, and free."

It seems so plain, so obvious,
how could I feel ill-fated?
To surround myself with the very best
that ever were created.

A friendship now days known by few,
the very best companions.
Contented just to pack us through
the mountains, plains, and canyons.

It seems forever, more or less,
he's shouldered mankind's loads
and brought us through the wilderness
with little use for roads.

And while I'm no religious man,
it must show good behavior
to be chosen as delivery van
and guardian of the savior.

He provides us with solutions
for problems yet uncounted,
but his greatest contributions
are not when he is mounted.

When you gaze upon a grazing jack,
you may see a lowly ass.
You can be sure he's looking back

'neath the guise of nibbling grass.

He wears the perfect poker face,
he is what you impose.
But while you stand there heels in place,
he's always on his toes.

Unknowing eyes will think they feast
upon a silly creature.
A simple, strange, and awkward beast
without redeeming feature.

Those that are demanding
will find his every fault
and take each patient standing
as a personal assault.

If then they try to use some force
and find he can't be budged.
He's judged the wrong end of a horse,
themselves correctly judged.

But patient, understanding eyes
might find a lifelong friend,
one to trust when hard times rise,
one to count on to the end.

So, if you see a lowly ass,
then that's just what he'll be
when viewing nature's looking glass,
you are just what you see.

Introduction

I've always wanted to be a cowboy but felt that I was born in the wrong place and at the wrong time. Being raised in the suburbs of university towns was hardly conducive to finding my life on the range. But from an early age, I always managed to find my way around to the horse crowd. From our family cabin near Allenspark, Colorado in the mountains of Boulder County, where we spent the long summers provided by the schedules of university professors, I wandered, as a pre-teen, to the local livery stable and hung around until I was finally put to work. By my junior high school years, I'd found my way to a Black Angus and Quarter Horse breeding farm on the outskirts of Iowa City, where I toughened up by bucking hay during the summer and feeding cattle and helping to break horses after school for the rest of the year.

The horses were all handraised, gentle, for the most part, and easy to get started under saddle. The owner would saddle and longe a horse until it calmed down and seemed controllable before having me climb on for some more longeing. Young horses are often longed, which is working them in a circle on a long lead. As soon as they started longeing smoothly and stopping on command, we would take them out on a pasture, dallied up on a fairly short lead at first, and then riding loose. It was rare to have one buck and those that did weren't much of a challenge to stay on. Young horses generally don't know how to buck very well. I was often out loping around with fairly good control within an hour or two of first having saddled the horse.

Although it was all very simple and easy, it made me feel like a rough and tough, experienced cowboy. I was certain that I was being used for my skill and competence. Having been to Larry Jo's kids' camp when I was still young enough to wet my saddle, and having talked my parents into a few riding lessons since then, I thought I was quite the expert. To my boss, however, I was merely someone dumb enough to do whatever he told me to, and young and athletic enough to probably not get hurt in the process. Overconfident ignorance became somewhat of a repeating theme that has led to many of the best adventures of my life.

Beyond work, I also tended to gravitate toward the farm crowd socially. My best friend/worst enemy alternately throughout high school was a farm kid named Jim Walker. Because we both had the first name Jim, we were always referred to as Duke and Walker, titles that, like our friendship, have lasted a lifetime. It was at his farm that I learned to hunt, pluck and butcher chickens, and ride pigs. The first animal to buck me off was a huge boar hog, which proved to be the toughest and most adventurous ride of my life. After sneaking up for a flying mount, you sat on the highest and widest point on the pig with absolutely nothing to hang onto. Upon falling off, you were guaranteed to land in pig shit which, to make matters worse, provided little traction as you tried to escape the angry boar. And once you'd managed to sail headfirst out of the pig pen, you had to quickly regain your feet to keep running before Walker's large father, who strongly disapproved of pig riding, discovered the cause of all his pigs squealing.

Texas

As a generally distracted and poor student, I eventually dropped out of high school and headed to Texas to pursue my cowboy dreams—and to provide my parents with a little of the well-deserved peace and quiet they couldn't enjoy while I was raising cane around town. My academically oriented parents actually encouraged me to drop out and leave, not because they didn't care, but because they knew it to be the only solution for any of us. And while my moving to Texas undoubtedly provided my folks with some well-deserved peace and quiet, it did little to help me settle down and grow up.

If part of the qualifications for being a cowboy involves being a social misfit, then I was at least partly qualified. While I had always been somewhat socially awkward, trying to mingle with the Texas cowboy crowd as a longhaired, bearded Yankee confirmed this image. And the farther I got from Austin, a liberal stronghold even back in the seventies, the greater the contrast between myself and the surrounding society. When I started working on a ranch near Wallis, about forty miles west of Houston, I might as well have been from a different planet.

By that time, Walker had graduated from high school and had come down to Texas to check out the ranch life. While we both hired on with the same "ranch investment firm," he had been assigned to a place near La Grange when I was moved to Wallis so I was mostly on my own. That was probably just as well because we tended to cause more commotion and get in more trouble when egging each other on in our mutual poor judgement.

The ranch consisted of a couple thousand acres along the Brazos River, small by the dry, rocky West Texas standards but huge by East Texas standards, where fertile farms and ranches were more often described in terms of scores, or maybe hundreds of acres. With white snowy egrets flying around or following the exotic-looking Brahman cattle on the upper pastures, and the dark, vine- and moss-covered live oak woodlands around the river bottom sloughs, filled with alligators, water moccasins, and alligator garfish, this was a wild new world to me. Still fresh from the cornfields of Iowa, I felt like I was in deepest, darkest Africa.

And as foreign as all this seemed to me, I apparently seemed even more foreign to all the local inhabitants. This small rural community rarely encountered Yankees even passing through, much less a long-haired hippie sort of Yankee who fancied himself to be a cowboy and who apparently planned to stay a while. To them I WAS from a different planet. A planet way to hell and gone up north called Ohio, or was it Idaho? No matter. Anything that far from Texas might as well have been in outer space.

My boss, a man named Benny Mize, was the pillar of the community. He was built like a pillar too; square and stout. His jaw was square and his hands were large, work-swollen blocks, each supporting five smaller pillars for fingers. He enjoyed extending his large, square hand out to me, palm up, to display some small treasure, maybe an arrowhead he had just found or some sort of ranching artifact or curious fossil, whatever. He would then slowly close his hand as a slight smile creased his chiseled face in a challenge to try to remove this valuable item from his iron grip. He would keep his eyes locked on mine to reiterate the challenge as he slowly transferred the treasure into his front pocket before returning to work, usually building or repairing fence.

I lived in Wallis for a relatively short time and never realized how important the town, and especially Benny Mize, had been in my life, until forty years later when I received a text message from my sister, Peg, in Austin.

The text message simply said, *"Benny Mize died."*

"Benny Mize died." I can't remember the last time three words have had that much impact. The memories, emotions, and confusion all caught me by surprise. I couldn't remember the last time Benny had even crossed my mind and never realized what an important figure he had been in my life. Benny Mize dead? It just didn't seem possible. People like that don't die. But then again, he was already ancient last time I'd seen him some forty years ago. He must have been at least forty or fifty way back then. How could he still have been alive after all those years? But how could he be dead? I had the startling realization that I was much older than he had been the last time I saw him. Another impossibility. I tried to visualize Benny as a frail old man but couldn't get it to register.

I called my sister to only further confuse the situation. "Benny's daughter had specifically requested that you be notified," Peg told me. "Apparently he still talked about you in his later years." I shamefully tried to remember that Benny had even had a daughter, just to distract myself from the fact that I had remained in his life while I had let him slip from mine. While it was immediately obvious how important he had been to me, it was beyond concept that I'd had any impact at all on that immovable mass of man. I thought again of his iron grip. Benny never released anything. What I wouldn't have given to have visited him just once in all those years.

Benny had lived in Wallis several miles from the ranch and managed several other ranch properties, so would only show up intermittently. I lived alone on the two-thousand-some-odd-acre ranch in a house (ranch style, I guess) about a half mile past the locked gate on the highway. Although I had lived only two hours away in College Station eight years earlier, that was several lifetimes ago to a twenty-year-old (ten years is just a glance over my shoulder at my current age) so I was basically a newcomer, fresh from Iowa. The Brazos River frontage, with its armadillos snuffling around in the dirt in their nearsighted way, sometimes right up to my feet, to look me up and down and maybe sniff a couple times before zipping away with amazing speed, the mockingbirds singing constantly, but never repeating themselves, the rattlesnakes on the high ground, the cottonmouths down in the slough by the river, and the slow, muddy river itself were more wild, exotic, adventurous, and dangerous than anything I'd ever seen, and I loved having it practically all to myself.

As deacon of the church, Benny went through the motions of trying to save me, mostly by just cordially inviting me to church, but he wasn't the type to impose his beliefs on others, except for work ethics under his employment. Hands in pockets were rewarded with a cuff to the head as reminder that men must always have their hands out and ready to work or fight. Anyway, I could tell his heart wasn't really into getting me baptized. I preferred to think that he sort of liked me the way I was, heathen and all. But the rest of Wallis didn't seem to share this casual attitude and I could tell he was pressured to lure me into their clutches. They figured they had themselves a genuine heathen which made me somewhat of a contemporary issue. Not to mention the fact that I'd migrated practically around the world to wind up in their little community indicating that I was looking for change, maybe a revelation even, and it was obviously providence. At the very least I was lost, lonely, and young enough to be easy pickins for salvation. At the bottom of it all, however, was just a very friendly community trying to welcome an awkward stranger the best way they knew how.

I'd been there a couple weeks and had met Benny's side kick, James Steward, a semi-retired old rancher who also had a key to our gate (and every other gate in the county) and who took great pleasure in having a hippie friend to come harass. I had also met Benny's brother-in-law, Shorty, another part-time employee with the only other key to the gate that I was aware of. So, I was surprised to see a car coming down the drive late one afternoon after work. Benny and James drove trucks and Shorty didn't drive due to constant drunkenness.

I don't think they gave DWIs in that area in those days. Shorty had just about wrecked every vehicle he ever had access to, including tractors and such. He had run himself over with a tractor just a year or so before I moved there. Well, I guess he hadn't really run over himself as the tractor wasn't really moving forward, but was digging itself down, lodged against the foundation of an old fallen farmhouse he had run into. Shorty had managed to get dragged under a rear wheel as it dug itself down, yet somehow lived to walk haltingly and talk unhaltingly. As Benny's brother-in-law, Shorty was more of a social and religious obligation than he was an employee.

Anyhow, this was the first time I'd seen an unknown vehicle approach my ranch house. This wouldn't have been any kind of big deal except that I, having settled in and feeling comfortable with my situation, had decided to have my own little housewarming party and had just smoked a joint. I'm pretty sure it was the first time I'd ever smoked pot alone because I remember thinking of the old truism, "Drinking alone is the first sign of alcoholism." It made me feel deliciously old, wicked, and derelict—I was already developing adult problems and I couldn't even vote yet.

It's amazing how high one gets when alone and without the distraction of others to share one's joint with. This is especially true when one started running around in a panic trying to make sure all one's weed was hidden and that one looked and acted fairly normal, or at least not high as a kite, when walking out to greet… who the hell was this anyway? Having spotted this vehicle almost a half mile away over the flat, treeless terrain of the upper pasture, I had an eternity to work myself up to a frenzy as the car slowly crawled down the long, rutted, muddy two-track lane.

Could it be Benny, or maybe James, in a borrowed car or riding with someone else? Or maybe just Shorty with a friend? That would be the easiest option because they'd be too drunk to notice my condition. I desperately hoped this to be the case. As it inched closer, I saw that it was a fairly new Lincoln Continental. *That can't be good. No wonder they're going so slow. Who would ever try to drive a low rider like that down a muddy lane like this?* My panic increased as the car got close enough to make out the silhouettes of many heads. It was full. Who were they? I considered heading out the back door toward the woods down by the river. No, I had to get a hold of myself. They might have already seen me too. I'm sure I was very flushed and almost hyperventilating as I walked off the porch to greet them, trying my best to look calm, even bored, with the situation.

The sedan was crammed full with the entire Wallis Baptist Youth Organization. They were all about my age, late teens to early twenties. They ranged in character from the virgin daughter of the car's owner, who had never even been as far away as Houston, to local cowboys, and even included an ex-junkie from Houston, who was evidently put in the position of emissary and possibly translator to help break the ice with their new northern, hippie pagan. He seemed to be put in the lead position, being the most likely to be able to relate to me. Looking at me, I'm sure they were all pretty thrilled to have found a soul so obviously lost and needing to be saved.

After a little bit of very awkward conversation led mostly by the junkie and mostly about how messed up he, too, (subtle about my obvious situation) had been before finding Jesus, the virgin driver tried a different tact, saying Benny had mentioned that my dogs knew lots of really neat tricks. That at least gave me a familiar routine; bang bang play dead, walk on hind legs, balance food on nose until told to toss and catch it, jump up on my shoulders and balance piggyback, frisbee (hippie) tricks, etc. My accidental chocolate Labradoodle (I had been devastated seeing that pansy-assed black poodle hooked up to my prize yellow Lab, whose future litter had already made me wealthy in my dreams) was smart as a whip and picked up any trick I showed her. The way those folks were all way too inordinately impressed by this little show was about all I can remember from our impromptu little get together, which lasted eternally longer than had their initial approach down my lane, except that I'd also been cornered into accepting their invitation to the church's annual summer picnic the next week.

The picnic was pretty much a repeat of the WBYO visit at the ranch, except that it had lots of adults and good food and even some beer available. The beer was possibly an exception for my benefit (even though I was underage) as it was commented on more than once, usually in a joking fashion, and often in comparison to Lutheran picnics, where whiskey was apparently drunk from paper cups and soda cans rather than openly—they appeared very self-conscious about it. But I appeared to be a center of attraction and everyone wanted to see all the dog tricks and, again, seemed to be way overly impressed by them. It was like being in the circus. I was the freak show, my dogs the trained animal act.

I'm fairly sure that everyone there extended a personal invitation to please join them in church... maybe next Sunday? They also had Bible study and prayer meetings several times a week, in case I was interested. I couldn't help but notice that neither James Stewart nor Shorty were anywhere to be seen. James Stewart turned out to be no more a church goer than me, while Shorty, although rarely sober enough to reach the church on Sunday mornings, claimed to be very religious and was especially grateful for God's forgiving nature.

James Stewart was quite the character, always trying to be out of line with what he assumed would be my liberal, Yankee sensitivities, usually having to do with racial slurs, which he knew made me uncomfortable, but able to respond to almost anything inappropriately and with the greatest shock factor. He knew (as everyone except maybe Shorty knew) that I was nowhere near the cowboy I claimed to be and tried to act like, but was much less inhibited than others in teasing me about it.

A typical conversation might go as follows:

"Howdy, Mr. Stewart, how you doing today?"

"Well, not worth a damn, Duke. Why just this morning, I went to fart, and damned if I didn't shit my britches! What you bin doing 'ere lately, Duke? You got any them heifers stump broke yet? We gone be working cattle 'ere pretty soon and we gone need a few stump broke heifers."

I had no idea what he was talking about, but thought I would just bullshit my way through and figure it out as I went along. "No sir, Mr. Stewart. I've been working on it, but haven't had much time here lately."

James Stewart dragged this line of conversation out intermittently for several weeks without ever cracking a grin before I finally figured out that "stump broke" involved heifers backing up to a stump for a little barnyard sodomy.

Shorty was a small guy, probably about forty, but looked at least a hundred. Since I was from up north, he assumed my brain was pretty much a blank slate and was eager to teach me everything he knew. He encouraged questions, telling me that was the best way to learn, and using the example of a person missing a finger. "The first thing you're gonna ask that person is 'did it hurt?' on account a you ain't never had a finger cut off, so you don't know." He also gave me lots of practical advice for everyday living, such as, "If you smoke a pipe, always take it out of your mouth before starting a fight. God O Mighty! Thought I was gonna choke to death!" He encouraged me to avoid alcohol and especially not to try to run a bar with the help of a beautiful young wife. "Them places is the devil's playground!"

I once gave him a ride to go see his mostly estranged wife. I was very surprised to be introduced to a fairly attractive, middle-aged woman with very flirtatious eyes and mannerisms, knowing Shorty was oblivious. I was even more surprised to meet his son, a very handsome and athletic-looking, 240-pound sixteen-year-old of mixed race. Shorty appeared equally oblivious to the lack of resemblance, just another of many awkward little encounters I was starting to get used to.

Out of boredom, loneliness, and libido, I occasionally dropped in at the Hilltop Tavern located a ways out of town on a straight stretch of highway that appeared to be flat as a pool table (flatter than the pool table in the bar) to the distant horizons in either direction. It was there one evening that I was trying, drunk and desperate, to hit on the barmaid, the only potentially sinful young woman in town who was close to my age. Her eyes were slightly crossed and might have outnumbered her real teeth—anything to avoid stump-breaking heifers. To this day, I count my lucky stars to have been unsuccessful, but still have occasional nightmares anyway.

On that particular evening she'd asked, probably just to make conversation, but possibly as an employee of the bar, how old I was, to which I gave my rote answer, "Twenty-one." I'd forever looked much younger than I was, still occasionally being pulled over by cops who couldn't believe I was even sixteen, much less twenty, and so could never figure out how I ever got away with drinking in bars, which I'd done frequently for a couple years. I'd never had a fake ID, or usually even a real one for that matter. It probably had something to do with the fact that I was always alone, unusual for youngsters sneaking into bars, and maybe by virtue of my ridiculously youthful appearance itself. Folks might have figured that nobody looking so young would ever try to pass for twenty-one if they weren't, and probably thought I must have some congenital condition they didn't want to embarrass me about in front of others. Whatever the reason, nobody ever "carded" me in those days.

On that particular evening, however, after having given my rote answer of, "Twenty-one," I puzzled for a moment and then asked, "What day is it anyway?"

"Tuesday," she replied.

"No, I mean, what is the date today?"

"June 4th," she said.

"Shit! I really am twenty-one, it's my birthday!"

The few people in the bar all stopped whatever they were doing and looked at me. I was thinking I would probably be seeing a few free drinks sent my way but instead, the bar tender sauntered over and asked to see my driver's license, which as usual, I didn't have with me. He took my Lone Star longneck, set it behind the bar, and pointed at the door. Some party.

I made sure I'd found my driver's license before I ever went back to the Hilltop, but I never was able to generate much rewarding social interaction with anyone there. The only person who had much interest in me was some old cowboy who moved over next to me at the bar and seemed to want to talk but couldn't seem to figure out what he wanted to say. And he had a look of desperation in his eyes that brought to mind my efforts to flirt with the cross-eyed barmaid. I started to suspect that he was a very frustrated and ashamed homosexual ("closet gay" wasn't known terminology in those days), and he likely assumed that I, as a longhair, was one of those like-minded young men he'd heard about, and possibly the solution to his lifelong frustrated fantasies. Who knows?

Due to my young and lonely appearance, I'd been hit on more than my fair share in the bars of Austin, and I was a bit homophobic at that point in my life. At any rate, the old cowboy was pretty much a fixture at the bar and made it difficult to try to socialize with anyone else or even have a peaceful beer by myself. The Hilltop wasn't barrels of fun and laughter anyway, so it wasn't too hard to give up.

Sometime in the next couple weeks I must have gotten lonely—and horny—enough to accept one of my many invites to go to church. Everyone's heard about how wild preachers' daughters can be, and having been on a couple CYO (Christian Youth Organization) trips in high school (nothing to do with religion, just a free bus ride to ski at Lacrosse Wisconsin where hell does indeed freeze over), I'd witnessed how much wild action can go on with these good Christians. I would wager that, at least in those days, most young women lost their virginity on church sponsored excursions.

I'd seen a few beautiful "Southern belles" around town, but never in any sort of situation where a shy and insecure outsider like myself could have ever even spoken to them. This was compounded by the fact that I had no intention of getting married and settling down, as was the normal and acceptable mode in this region, and so carried the guilt and paranoia of someone just wanting to get laid. I assumed I was sufficiently transparent regardless of efforts to hide or disguise my illicit intentions that I might as well be carrying a neon sign over my head to advertise this.

Anyhow, I was desperate enough to go check out the church scene or, more specifically, the church girls. This turned out to be somewhat difficult with the entire church crowd all trying very hard to act like they weren't checking me out. While I tried to calm my paranoias, I could feel the tangible, subdued energies of expectation engulfing me from every direction. About a hundred hours into the service, the preacher, Jean Frank, was nearing the end of his sermon. I really hadn't paid attention to it while trying to sneak glances here and there at various young women, but the sermon had almost certainly been geared toward converting heathens. He paused to get everyone's (my) attention, launched his arms and face up to the heavens, and declared, "What a beautiful day for salvation."

He brought his hands and face back down, ever so slowly and silently for maximum effect, his eyes landing on mine, which immediately dropped down to inspect the tops of my boots. Long silence. "A beautiful day for salvation," he repeated. Slightly shorter silence. "Is there anyone among us wishing to cleanse their souls of sin?" Pause. "And open their hearts to Jesus?" Pause. "Then come forward and pray with me and ye shall be forgiven." Longest silence. Then first one, and then another person came to the front of the church to kneel and pray with Jean Frank (presumably pre-planned "stooges" to help show me what to do and provide company for the act).

From their lower vantage point and with their backs to the rest of us, their voices weren't as loud and clear but some "forgive me," and "I have sinned," and "thank you, Jesus" phrases could be heard by the rest of us. I risked a glance up to see Jean Frank standing over their bowed heads with one hand on each, his eyes still on me. I quickly looked back at my boots.

"Anyone," he repeated more loudly. "Anyone at all?" Several more joined the prayers up front. More mumbling emerged from among them as Jean moved about, touching bowed heads. "Would anyone else like to join us? Anyone at all?" A few more stepped forward, started to pray. "Or maybe you would like to renew your commitment to the Lord and share your love with Jesus. Come forward and pray with us!" Jean bellowed. More folks moved forward.

I glanced around just enough to realize I was sitting alone in the pews with everyone else up front praying. Jean was still staring at me and repeated in full volume now, "Anyone, anyone at all." As I sat there staring at my boots, wondering how long this standoff could last, I again considered the notion of eternity. Religion seemed to involve a lot of eternities.

They never did get me baptized. Benny never got involved in trying. But Benny did give me somewhat of a spiritual awakening, although he wasn't trying to. I don't remember him ever trying to give me any sort of advice or direction other than what was necessary for the job at hand. I really can't remember anything he said to me, but only his ways and how he accepted me as I was. And somehow in his quiet ways, he gave me a new faith in human nature and kindness. He became a keystone in my foundation of human understanding and the basic good in life in general. I miss him enough now to make up for the forty years I hadn't missed him at all.

The ranch in Wallis had little use for horses. The pastures were all easily accessible by truck, and the wooded bottom lands were so dense with brush and vines that they were barely accessible on foot, much less on horseback. We had a few horses nonetheless, but these were so spoiled and abused by the inexperienced ranch owners that they had a strong distaste and distrust of all humans. The owners consisted of a partnership of several "city slicker" types, some of whom were ex-pro football players, who invested in ranch properties to fix up for resale. The horses were there largely for appearances and for the occasional pleasure of the owners and their children, none of whom knew anything about horses.

The macho-minded ex-ball players in particular tended to be very heavy-handed to the point of being abusive. At that time, I didn't know enough about horses to either earn their trust or to correct their behavior, so the few times I attempted to ride resulted in continuous conflict with the poor beasts and wasn't much fun for any of us. It probably didn't help that the first time I rode any of them was also the first time I tried peyote. Walker had come to visit and had brought some peyote that he'd come across somewhere.

Neither of us knew how to clean it properly, resulting in both of us getting even sicker than what's normal with peyote. I'm pretty sure that my horse, named Screwy Louie for his erratic behavior, had never been puked off of before. Puking is a very extreme and unusual behavior and wasn't well received. All in all, it wasn't a good first experience with peyote for any of us and I'm sure that the horses, as sensitive as they are to our own moods and energies, weren't much pleased with our company. First impressions with critters are even more important than with other humans.

The only good horse experience I had while working for that outfit was when I was "loaned" to another ranch for fall roundup. This operation had some good cowponies and experienced hands who knew how to care for them. Being the newcomer, Yankee, and hippie, I was somewhere below the lowest rung of the ladder and was stuck with the last choice in horses. He was a scrawny little guy with hairy fetlocks and other characteristics of the original Spanish Barb breeds first introduced by Hernan Cortez in the sixteenth century, and the ancestors of the original wild (feral) mustangs. Initially disappointed at being stuck with so inglorious a mount, I soon developed the appropriate respect for that little guy. He had far more stamina than any of the larger horses and was barely beginning to break a sweat in the heat of the day while the other horses were thoroughly lathered. Although we did the widest sweep around the ranch and covered more ground than anyone else, he was still going strong long after the large, muscular Quarter Horses were played out to the point of stumbling along.

I have been partial to these smaller breeds ever since. These breeds were the backbone of the American West. These were the ponies that could withstand the rigors of long-distance travel over the rough country encountered on cattle drives. Even then, each cowboy required a string of about half a dozen horses to rotate through. Andy Adams's book, *The Log of a Cowboy*, does an excellent job of describing the value of such horses in the harsh conditions of a cattle drive. The book, first published in 1903, is considered by historians to be one of the most accurate first-hand accountings of an actual cattle drive.

I occasionally got over to La Grange to visit Walker and check out his ranch situation. At that time, La Grange was still home to the most famous whore house in the south. It pre-dated the American Civil War and was called the "Chicken Ranch" because during the post-war poverty years, they began accepting chickens as payments and eventually started raising chickens and eggs as a side business. ZZ Top wrote a fairly well-known song called "La Grange" about that whore house.

Walker and I always had big plans to visit that whore house and always came up with weak excuses, not wanting to admit that we were too chicken to go to the Chicken

Ranch. It wound up getting closed down in 1973, before we could ever build up the courage to give it a try. It was a terribly ugly scene when some glory-seeking goddam Yankee reporter embarrassed local officials into reluctantly shutting down their proud historic landmark that was claimed to have entertained more politicians than had the state capital. The story hit the front pages of many national magazines. It hit national news again several months later, when the same reporter returned for a follow-up story and was severely beaten by the sheriff, apparently one of many elected officials invested in the business.

Although we never made it to the Chicken Ranch (or at least never made it from the parking lot to the front door), we did visit a whore house south of the border. One of our wealthy bosses had a high dollar bird dog that he wanted to have bred to some champion bird dog located down close to the border. I volunteered for the trip and Walker couldn't help but tag along. After having dropped off the bitch in heat and having miraculously survived a thorough vehicle search near the border, we stashed our weed and stuff and ventured into Mexico.

Our experience was likely the same as with any young men in that situation and didn't get too interesting until we tried driving back across the border. My beat-up old truck with two half-drunk cowboys was an obvious target for being searched. The border patrol officers brought their dog over to sniff for drugs and, upon smelling the bird dog's odor of being in heat all over the seat, the dog started going wild. Certain that my truck was about to be dismantled, I started trying to explain the situation to the border guard, but he merely laughed and said he could tell the difference. With the dog rendered ineffective, the manual search intensified, and I still worried about my truck being dismantled if they found seeds or other evidence.

Walker apparently didn't share my concerns and was feeling like a smart-ass. When a guard asked where we got the bale of hay in the pick-up bed, Walker replied that we'd stolen it from a poor old cow. I could have punched him, but the guard merely ignored him and cut the bale open to search through the contents. An hour or so later, we were back on the road and trying to remember where we'd left our stash. Although we'd used condoms, we both dosed ourselves heavily with antibiotics from my brother-in-law's veterinary clinic when we got home.

That was our last trip to Mexico together and the last errand we did for our wealthy bosses. It turned out that our "city slicker" ranch owners were as crooked as suggested by their company name, "Captain Credit Cattle Company," and the whole operation went broke with a couple owners even doing time behind bars. One summer in the heat and humidity of the Houston countryside was plenty enough for me, and I was glad to get back to work at my brother-in-law's ranch near Paige, Texas. While not nearly as humid as the Brazos river bottom near Wallis, the summers were still pretty brutal and I became migratory, feeding cattle during the winter when my help was most needed and heading north to work at a guest ranch in Colorado in the summers.

While I did enjoy ranch work and especially working cattle, branding, castrating, and vaccinating during spring and fall roundups, much of the time in between could be pretty lonely and boring. I was forced to face the fact that I wasn't the loner I'd always fancied myself to be and wanted to be, but was instead a very social type. The main factor leading me away from ranching, however, was the realization that horses, not cattle, were my true passion. Maybe if I'd worked on a big spread in West Texas or another area where most of the work was done from horseback, I would have remained a cowboy forever. As it was, however, I found myself drifting away from the ranching life and more toward the wrangling life—or anything that involved working with equines.

Meanwhile, I'd discovered a by-product of the cattle business that provided me with some contraband on my northern journeys.

http://wbp.bz/donkeys

HOT NEW RELEASES

PRECIOUS FEW CLUES
http://wbp.bz/precious

FIELDS OF FORTUNE
http://wbp.bz/fortune

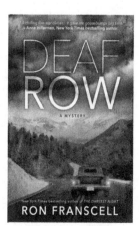

DEAF ROW
http://wbp.bz/deafrow

Made in United States
North Haven, CT
24 January 2024

47892027R00104